Zero Karat

Zero Karat

The Donna Schneier Gift to the American Craft Museum

With essays by Ursula Ilse-Neuman and David Revere McFadden

American Craft Museum   New York 2002

American Craft Museum

40 West Fifty-third Street

New York, New York 10019

Zero Karat: The Donna Schneier Gift to the American Craft Museum

May 30–September 9, 2002

Organized by Ursula Ilse-Neuman, Curator, American Craft Museum

Editor: Nancy Preu

Catalogue Designer: Martin Pálka

Installation Designer: Rupert Deese

Graphic Designer: Michael Batista

ISBN 1-890385-08-5

Library of Congress Control Number 2002104344

Printed in the Czech Republic by Real Tisk Prague.

Photo Credits

Figs. 1, 2,3, 4, and 6 courtesy of the Museum Het Kruithuis; fig 5 courtesy of Gijs Bakker; figs. 7 and 8 photo by Bob Cramp; fig. 9 photo by David Poston; fig. 10 photo by David Ward; fig. 11 photo by Lux Feininger, © 2002 The Oskar Schlemmer Theatre Estate, I-288824, Oggebio, Italy.

Photographs of objects in the catalogue are by Martin Tůma, except for the following: nos. 6, 26, 27, 32, 35, and 44 photo by Eva Heyd, New York; no. 20 photo by David Ward.

Photographs of the artists are courtesy of the artists, except for that of Douglas Fuchs, which is courtesy of the American Craft Council. The following photographers are credited for their photographs: Ton Werkhoven (Gijs Bakker); Chris Van Houts, Amsterdam (Peter Chang); Cary Okazaki (Arline Fisch); Hardie Truesdale (David Freda); Gordon Bakker (Lisa Gralnick); Ian Douglas Vollmer (Laurie Hall); Dan Burn-Forti (Susanna Heron); Michael Dames (Otto Künzli); Paul Clemens, Bad Neuenahr, Germany, 2002 (Wilhelm Mattar); Fin Serck-Hanssen (Michael Petry); Doug Hagley (Hiroko Sato-Pijanowski); Carol Hinote (Gene Pijanowski); Paul Barrow (Wendy Ramshaw); Mark Fincher (Marjorie Schick); Miranda Watkins (David Watkins).

Contents

FOREWORD

The American Craft Museum has long been committed to the display and interpretation of contemporary jewelry. *Zero Karat* represents a benchmark in this history. The publication and the exhibition mark the Museum's acquisition of the Donna Schneier collection, one of the largest and most important in this field to date, and affirm the Museum's commitment to collect contemporary jewelry and chronicle the history of this vital art form as it unfolds.

We are indeed indebted to Donna Schneier for her generosity and vision. It was through her passion for and commitment to contemporary jewelry that this collection came into existence at a time when most of the jewelers represented in it were still relatively unknown. She had the courage to collect art that was daring and bold, some pieces of which would have been lost altogether had they not entered her collection. Her work as an advocate for contemporary jewelry artists continues to this day.

Donna Schneier's long-standing relationship with the American Craft Museum encouraged her to donate her collection for public education. Her gift supports the Museum's determination to be a center for the study of twentieth- and twenty-first–century jewelry and constitutes a cornerstone addition to our permanent collection, both in its range and in its quality. It is my great pleasure to thank Donna Schneier for all that she has done to help the American Craft Museum in its goal to record and interpret the history of this extraordinary form of artistic expression.

The Donna Schneier collection comprises landmark objects from a pivotal and intriguing period in the history of twentieth-century jewelry. The introduction of non-precious materials in the post-War era marked a profound change in the perception of the art form and questioned the role of jewelry and personal adornment in contemporary society. Using aluminum, rubber, plastic, newspaper, and even clothespins, the jewelry artists represented in *Zero Karat* created innovative and beautiful works that communicate the significance of ideas, design, and execution. They challenged the traditional view that the value of jewelry resided primarily in the intrinsic value of its raw materials, and their experimentation opened the door to a vibrant new form of object making and a new interpretation of the meaning of jewelry.

Several people at the American Craft Museum should be singled out for their work in bringing this project to fruition. Curator Ursula Ilse-Neuman worked tirelessly, initially on the acquisition of the objects and then as coordinator of the catalogue and exhibition. Her catalogue essay on the evolution of Dutch and British jewelry between 1965 and 1985 is a major contribution to the study of contemporary jewelry and adds to her other accomplishments in this field. We are thankful for her oversight and insights. Chief Curator David McFadden's essay on the production of jewelry in America and other countries during this period also adds original research to the field. The American Craft Museum is grateful to both curators for their expertise.

Our thanks go to curatorial assistant Jennifer Scanlan, who participated in virtually every phase of the project, and curatorial intern Ellen Dodington, as well as to Nancy Preu for her sensitive editing and advice during the assembly of the catalogue. Exhibition designer Rupert Deese must be thanked for conceiving an innovative installation that displays the works to their best advantage.

We are also grateful to our friends and colleagues in the Czech Republic who worked with Donna Schneier and the American Craft Museum on this publication: Martin Pálka for design, Martin Tůma for photography, and Pavel Opočenský for coordinating the many tasks involved in its production in Prague.

Finally, I thank those of our Collections Committee who always work enthusiastically to help build the American Craft Museum's collection, especially Simona Chazen and Mark Grainer, who co-chair the committee. I am particularly grateful to the Board of Governors, to Chairman Barbara Tober, and to President Nan Laitman for their support as we expand and enrich the collection in the twenty-first century.

Holly Hotchner
Director

COLLECTOR'S STATEMENT

Do we follow certain paths in life because we have chosen them or because fate has chosen them for us? In 1985, I took the American Craft Museum's Collectors Circle trip to England. At the time, I owned a traditional commercial jewelry business, and I was looking forward to seeing an exhibition of contemporary crafts at the British Crafts Centre in London. That trip and that exhibition were my introduction to progressive and avant-garde developments in jewelry.

The work on display at the British Crafts Centre had been made for the reasons all art is made: to explore, to celebrate, and to question. I was intrigued by what I saw and came home with eleven pieces of jewelry. That was the start of my collection, and it also marked the beginning of many cherished associations and friendships with contemporary jewelry artists, collectors, and museum and gallery personnel who share my enthusiasm for this exciting art form.

Most of the jewelry that I acquired would take courage to wear. My office walls in New York City were bare back in 1985, so armed with a graduate degree in art history and accountable only to myself, I installed my collection on my office walls. I enjoyed looking at and thinking about these forms, and I continued, over the years, to add new pieces to my collection. Some of the objects I acquired were seminal to the history of twentieth-century jewelry, and over time the collection evolved into a document of "revisionist" thinking in jewelry.

It has always been my understanding that artists make their work for posterity. For however long we as individuals are caretakers of their work it is but a brief time in the history of art. Art is meant to be shared. The most I can do as an appreciator of art is to help this process along. Art has been good to me. It is now my turn to be good to art.

I thank my husband, Leonard Goldberg; the American Craft Museum's director, Holly Hotchner; its curators, David McFadden and Ursula Ilse-Neuman; and my friend Pavel Opočenský for the opportunity to present my contribution to the history of twentieth-century jewelry.

Donna Schneier

Magic in the Mundane: Jewelry from the Donna Schneier Collection

David Revere McFadden

Paper, tin, wire, wood, rubber, plastic—the unremarkably ordinary contents of junk drawers, tool boxes, and wastebaskets around the world, and yet, in the hands of an artist, these humble and mundane materials can be transformed into memorable and engaging works of art.

The Donna Schneier collection of jewelry, a generous gift to the American Craft Museum, adds significantly to the Museum's existing collection of art jewelry made by international artists of the twentieth and twenty-first centuries. The unique qualities of the Schneier collection—specifically its focus on works of non-precious and alternative materials, as well as recycled or found objects—make it an invaluable reference for the study of trends in jewelry design that began in the 1960s and culminated in the 1980s, at a time of change and innovation in the field. Highlighting memorable and influential works by jewelry artists from the Netherlands, Great Britain, the United States, Germany, Poland, Czechoslovakia, and Norway, the Schneier collection documents the continuing evolution of the "jewelry as art" movement launched earlier in the twentieth century by such artists as Picasso, Calder, Braque, and Bertoia. On another level, the collection sounds a clarion note in the ongoing story of jewelry and body adornment, one that signals the artistic goals and concerns of a younger generation of creators, innovators who tested the boundaries that traditionally separated jewelry design from sculpture. A new vision of jewelry was proposed by these artists, one that turned traditional hierarchies of artistic and economic value upside down. What started as a minor revolution quickly overtook the mainstream of international jewelry design during these decades.

In his engaging and outré novel *Jewelry Talks* (2001), Richard Klein muses on the origins of ornamental jewelry in the Greek word *cosmos*. In its grandest sense, the word describes an entire universe. From the same word, however, is derived both a noun and an adjective—*cosmetic*—which Klein defines as "the most exterior, inessential, frivolous, superficially decorating without essentially transforming the self." *Ornamental* and *decorative* are also words that function on two levels, connoting either a uniquely human intervention in the way that things of the world appear or, by contrast, things of little true value or significance, entirely forgettable. And probably nowhere in the visual arts do the concepts of ornament and value intersect more visibly than in the world of jewelry.

The history of jewelry as ornamentation for the body has been written along two separate but often intersecting lines documenting two different streams of development in the field. One stream of development, the historically dominant one, has been established according to the criterion of intrinsic value. Precious metals such as gold, silver, and platinum, or prized stones that range from brilliant diamonds to midnight sapphires, embody economic value. The possession and control of these rare materials can buttress the economies of entire societies. When worn by individuals, these same materials become publicly visible forms of currency, bank accounts that are on display and ready for social, cultural, or financial transactions. As Richard Klein bluntly states it, "Diamonds will buy you lunch in any diner in the world." Power is encoded in the materials themselves. The ways in which the materials are used, transformed, or combined offers glimpses into individual personality and taste.

A second tributary in the history of jewelry can be traced in the use of non-precious materials that have been magically transformed by an artist, craftsman, or designer into something of value that transcends the materials themselves. From ancient Egyptian ceramic pastes frits that emulated precious and semi-precious stones to the rich and vibrant enamels of the Middle Ages, or from the brilliantly cut glass-pastes of eighteenth-century Portugal and England to the stamped gutta-percha and woven hair jewelry of the nineteenth century, such jewels assumed their worth through their associative and aesthetic values, which were recognized by the innovative artists who created them and revealed through the quality of workmanship required to make the mundane into the magical. Through art, the artifice becomes complete.

Discussions of the inherent and associated values of materials have been critical to the understanding of art of the twentieth century in general, with specific implications for the history of modern and contemporary jewelry. It seems apparent that there is a gap between the values assigned to materials and the value of creativity as it is used to transform raw materials into objects of value. The truth of this hypothesis is reflected in the tax laws of the United States; an artist who donates a work to a museum or other non-profit institution may claim a tax deduction only on the materials used to make the work. This leads one to assume that our government deems creative ideas and skilled workmanship to be valueless even when embodied in a work of art. What then happens when great ideas are manifested in valueless and mundane materials? Does the magic of art transcend the limitations of the mundane? When photographer Edward Steichen sought to import Constantin Brancusi's *Bird in Space* into the United States in 1928 as a work of art, and hence not subject to duty, the United States Customs Service refused, classifying the sculpture as a "manufactured item. composed wholly or in chief value of iron, steel, lead, copper, brass, pewter, nickel, zinc, aluminum or other metal" (Steiner 2001: 19–25). Even though Steichen eventually prevailed in his lawsuit to get the opinion overturned, the case raised important issues of how the value of a work of art is to be determined and how creativity is to be acknowledged as a meaningful component of value.

The Schneier collection is a case study in the changing nature of art and design as reflected in the artists' choices of materials. Not only did artists prefer non-precious metals—copper, tin, and steel—over gold and silver, but they also looked toward a broader range of mundane materials than ever before, including wood, plastics, and paper. Out of the choices made by jewelry artists in this era grew a distinct and highly developed vocabulary of abstract forms and specialized techniques that contributed to a new sensibility of jewelry as a form of public theater.

The role of Dutch and British artists in formulating a new jewelry aesthetic in response to larger cultural, social, political, and economic changes has been admirably discussed in Ursula Ilse-Neuman's essay in this book. The powerful influence of the Dutch and British innovators cannot be overestimated in any study of alternative jewelry design in the rest of the world, and especially in the United States. In one sense the circle was completed: the impact of American Abstract Expressionism in Europe from the 1950s onward was echoed in a return influence in the world of jewelry design. The circular nature of these influences, as documented in the Schneier collection, makes the study of jewelry in the period particularly rewarding. Viewed against the backdrop of developments in the Netherlands and England, works by American, German, Swiss, and Norwegian artists take on new meaning. These artists contributed their own vision to the changing landscape of jewelry design, utilizing an astonishing array of materials and unorthodox forms.

If there is one theme that pervades much of the jewelry in the Schneier collection during the three decades surveyed, it is in the artists' conscious choice of alternative materials to express emotional and psychological states of being, as well as more formal visual qualities. Elements of surprise, humor, and irony are conveyed through the combination of materials and forms. In other works a sense of discomfort is created by juxtaposing intimate and sensual ornaments for the body with the implied danger of certain materials. Many of these works gain their power of engagement through the ambivalent or mixed messages they convey. Clearly these are works that are animated by contact with the human body; their meaning is derived, in fact, from their relationships to the geography of the human form, whether to the wrist, the neck, or the hand. And the messages of these pieces are underscored or revealed through the specific materials of which they are made.

Probably closest in spirit to traditional jewelry are the works made of metals. Whereas jewelers traditionally had relied on silver, gold, and platinum to reassert the sensuality and tactility of the body, these new artists found a strange beauty and the potential to suggest subjective states of being in industrial metals such as aluminum and tin. Polish-born Israeli artist Esther Knobel, who trained at the Royal College of Art in London, created an extended series of ambiguous cookie-cutter brooches with figures engaged in aggressive or defensive postures (see nos. 22–24). Made of flattened sheets of tin with raw edges, Knobel's "tin soldiers" are brightly painted with patterns that disguise their actions; the paint hides the material, metaphorically disguising the combat occurring on the battlefront of the wearer's body.

A similar sense of threat and danger is also conveyed through the crudely cut forms and sharp edges of the tin disks that make up Wilhelm Mattar's *Coca-Cola Nivea Necklace* of 1982 (see no. 31). Cut from commercial tin cans, the disks of this necklace are pierced and strung together on simple wire strands, with no attempt to disguise their polluted origins as trash. The necklace, when worn, produces a thin rattling sound, reminding the wearer of the mundane origins of the materials.

Arline Fisch's *Cuff (MKB67)* (see no. 13) is a complex machine-knitted structure in jewel-like tones of blue and purple. Part of the artist's continuing investigation of textile techniques, this woven cuff slides over the hand to encircle the wrist seamlessly. The delicate, lace-like quality of the knitted structure belies the industrial strength of the metal wires. While the cuff appears to drape the wrist in foamy and light-reflective color, it is also suffocating, densely intertwined, and complicated. In its radiance and sparkle, the work has a darker underside, much like a beautiful but poisonous sea anemone that envelops the wearer's wrist.

Nothing in Otto Künzli's jewelry occurs by chance, particularly his choice of materials. Künzli's *Ring for Two* from 1980 (see no. 26) exploits the sheen, tensile strength, and permanence of stainless steel to reiterate with a single structure the binding of two individuals. Not only does the ring serve as a symbolic and physical link between two individuals, it also proclaims in a blatant and public manner the erosion of individual freedom that comes with relationships. Künzli carefully weighs our expectation about materials against reality in his famous rubber *Gold Makes You Blind* bracelet, also from 1980 (see no. 27). The industrial black rubber tube is swollen at a single point, an effect created by the insertion of a gold sphere inside the rubber. For Künzli, the bracelet is a metaphor for the magical material of gold itself, which comes shining from the ground after millions of years in the darkness. The social, economic, and scientific history of gold has added to its legendary luster. Künzli felt that gold had lost its artistic value, and through this gesture returned gold to the underground darkness of the black rubber bracelet.

These works, and others in the Schneier collection, underscore the belief that materials are never neutral but carry with them associations that give them enhanced value beyond the economic. For Norwegian artist Liv Blåvarp, wood—a material generally associated with furniture and architecture—is the medium of choice for her complex structures. Held in close proximity to the skin by way of internal elastic bands, Blåvarp's bracelet (see no. 2) becomes an extension of the skin and flesh. By way of contrast,

Marjorie Schick's colorful painted wood structures—exuberant, spiky, and architectural—assume a more provocative and challenging position vis-à-vis the body (see nos. 40–41). Their sharp angles and outsized proportions stand in unresolved opposition to the soft and organic body upon which they are displayed. Schick's jewels, like gaudily painted wooden construction sets, exist in a zone somewhere between playful toys and threatening weapons.

The work of Czech sculptor Pavel Opočenský (see no. 32) privileges materials that are located somewhere on the spectrum between the rare and the ordinary. The artist is recognized for his powerful simple forms, but also for his ability to make the most unlikely materials interact with light. This magic is achieved by carving and polishing opaque materials—stone, bone, ivory, or even sections cut from laminated snow skis—to a thinness that makes them translucent or gives them the sheen of fine silk. In Opočenský's hands the most intractable and ordinary of materials takes on new life, an animation that derives from the transformative power of light.

Paper, string, and fiber were used as primary materials by many artists working in the 1980s, a phenomenon well documented in the Schneier collection. Traditional Japanese gilded paper cord *(mizuhiki)* was used by Hiroko Sato-Pijanowski and Gene Pijanowski to make a theatrical neckpiece and bracelet (see no. 35) that resemble mezzaluna chopping knives, or sickle-like blades, that rest precariously on the neck or wrist. Ironically, the suggested danger of the shapes, not to mention the physical and cultural weight of gold, was given tangible form in this most harmless of materials.

Robert Ebendorf has been at the forefront of art jewelry in the United States for nearly four decades. Following his studies at the University of Kansas from 1954 to 1963, Ebendorf received a Fulbright Fellowship that permitted him to travel and study in Norway. By the late 1960s, Ebendorf had evolved a personal style that made extensive use of the most mundane of materials, ranging from cheaply printed, tissue-thin Chinese newspaper (see no. 10) to everyday wooden spring-loaded clothespins combined with shards of industrial laminate (see no. 11). Ebendorf's idiosyncratic selection and juxtaposition of found or recycled materials in works that praise the commonplace is still, however, informed by his ongoing interest in the definition of beauty. Ebendorf's castoff wrapping papers, glued around lightweight spheres, are juxtaposed with passages of 24k gold foil—a reminder of the seductive appeal of the precious. Ebendorf's work offers a new definition of beauty that combines elements of surprise in the recognition of the ordinary with the reassurance of the eternally beautiful.

Transformation of the mundane into the magical has been a hallmark of Verena Sieber-Fuchs's work since the 1980s. Beginning as a textile artist, Sieber-Fuchs brought her skills in creating complex structures to bear in her jewels. Over her long and distinguished career working in alternative materials, Sieber-Fuchs has made use of Styrofoam, torn paper, wires, bandage and pill wrappings, egg cartons, wine bottle corks, firecrackers, and candies. In her work, Sieber-Fuchs pushes the limits of the non-precious to the very edge by including materials that have a limited life expectancy. The magic of her designs and their ability to engage our eyes and imaginations are best compared to the experience of live theater, during which observers "willingly suspend their disbelief" to participate in the magic. By praising the mundane for its unique beauty, Sieber-Fuchs reminds us that we are the source of the limitations on our imaginations. She emphasizes this further when she selects materials that carry powerful social, cultural, and political meanings. Sieber-Fuchs's *Apart-heid* necklace (see no. 43), a lush and tactile froth of translucent pink tissue, is comprised of hundreds of wrapping papers for oranges exported from racist South Africa. With one powerful gesture, the artist brings us from the magical world of the imagination to the harshest of mundane realities.

In its rich diversity of materials, forms, and techniques, the Schneier collection remains an important documentary resource for students and scholars interested in the evolution of modern jewelry. For everyone it is an engaging library of surprises that gives us reason to examine and appreciate the potential magic that lives just below the surface of our everyday world.

None that Glitters:
Perspectives on Dutch and British Jewelry in the Donna Schneier Collection

Ursula Ilse-Neuman

The works in the Donna Schneier collection are representative of the eventful years from 1965 to 1985 when major political, social, and economic changes in Europe, Great Britain, and the United States led to revolutionary changes in jewelry design. In a declaration of independence, young jewelry artists asserted that ideas, creativity, and inventiveness were to be the criteria by which jewelry would be judged in the new, rapidly changing society. Using non-precious materials such as aluminum, rubber, plastic, and paper to emphasize their liberation from past values and influences, these artists set a course of exploration that continues to make contemporary jewelry visually and conceptually exciting to this day.[1]

The decision to use raw materials of little intrinsic value was central to the campaign that these young jewelers were waging, ensuring that the value of a piece of jewelry would derive from the quality of the artist's ideas, design, and craftsmanship, just as in the fine arts, the cost of materials was of little significance to the importance of the work of art itself.[2] In their explorations, the creators of the new jewelry considered issues that were under investigation in the fine arts such as geometric abstraction, minimalism, and performance art. In addition, they took a deep interest in the social, economic, and technological changes that were transforming and democratizing society. The status, wealth, and power that defined the parameters of the field historically held no sway with these crusaders. Their ideas were political as well as artistic, and they were interested in reaching a wider public than the traditional small circle of wealthy patrons. They sought a new form of expression that helped to redefine jewelry, the relationships between maker and wearer, and jewelry's role in the marketplace.

The production of jewelry in non-precious materials is traceable to fundamental changes in Western society in the decades following the end of the Second World War. This era witnessed major improvements in the quality of life for the middle class, growing opportunities for education and travel, and the increasing ability for a broader section of the population to acquire nonessential goods and influence fashion trends and the economy.

As Western Europe rebuilt after the Second World War, the influence of American popular culture and the success of the American economy had a profound impact on the course of its recovery. Europeans were interested in the American lifestyle, but not in a slavish acceptance of it. For them, "Americanization" meant adapting and incorporating the products of American culture into their lives. In the process, these imports were substantially transformed. Because Americans were not subject to class distinctions that were as rigid as those in Europe, Europeans perceived the American lifestyle as one that emphasized innovation and mobility extending beyond the economic sphere to social and cultural life. In their minds, American cultural life was characterized by freedom, informality, liberality, vitality, modernity, and youthfulness.

One of the most remarkable changes after the Second World War was the emergence, first in the United States and then in Europe and Great Britain, of young people as consumers with enough financial power to exert a strong influence on popular culture, notably on music and fashion. This younger generation was less constrained by tradition, and their rejection of the accepted practices and lifestyles of their elders became a dominant theme in the 1960s and 1970s. Throughout this period, the younger generation helped wage class struggles and political and economic battles against traditional attitudes and practices in much of the Western world.

Artists from many countries contributed to the revolution in jewelry design that began in the 1960s by working individually as artists rather than as designers for large-scale fabrication. In the United States, university programs and art schools fostered an independent jewelry tradition starting in the late 1950s and early 1960s. The most influential elements in establishing the new international art jewelry movement, however, came from Europe, where dramatic departures were taken from long and distinguished goldsmithing traditions. Joining the political and artistic vanguard, accomplished goldsmiths deliberately violated accepted practices to encourage individuality and expressiveness as an antidote to anonymous technical perfection.

A NEW EPICENTER
The Netherlands and Great Britain, neither of which had been considered influential centers for jewelry prior to the 1960s, were to become the crucibles for the most far-reaching explorations in jewelry design in the twentieth century. Concentrating on the developments in art, craft, fashion, and popular culture in these countries over the course of twenty years, from 1965 to 1985, brings out the essential ideas and interactions that are reflected in the jewelry designed during this exciting time of great transition.

The development of jewelry made of non-precious materials took place most rapidly and decisively in the Netherlands. Almost unique among European countries, the Netherlands had an egalitarian society that could be traced back to the sixteenth century. With its enormous prosperity following the discovery of natural gas in the North Sea in 1959, the Netherlands was in an exceptionally strong position to extend its democratic predilections into a social agenda for the entire society. The revenues that flowed into the government allowed the Dutch to adopt wide-reaching social welfare legislation with the goal of distributing the new wealth and creating an egalitarian state. As a result, with less to protest from an economic perspective than their counterparts throughout Europe, Dutch youth focused their attention on restrictions on their self-expression.

The Dutch people began to grow accustomed to economic security as well as greater leisure time and "disposable income" in the 1950s. The conspicuous frugality and pronounced simplicity in personal appearance that had been encouraged by Dutch tradition were shunned by a younger generation that valued individuality and had the wherewithal to buy clothing and jewelry to express themselves. Beneficiaries of Holland's prosperity, the younger generation helped shape a new consumer society that rebelled against the constraints of Dutch conservatism.

During this period, the Dutch government played a key role in encouraging new art forms by providing support to artists and designers through programs and grants for education, exhibitions, and materials. This abundant government funding allowed jewelers the freedom to experiment with styles, materials, and techniques that might not have had a ready market. This was fundamentally different from the climate in Germany, where the democratic approach to jewelry making did not receive strong government support, and work in gold and precious materials remained predominant. Conditions were also fundamentally different in the United States, where many jewelers could support themselves through teaching positions but still had to be concerned with the realities of the marketplace.

Dutch Smooth

In the Netherlands in the late 1960s, a group led by goldsmith/designer Gijs Bakker (b. 1942) and his wife, the designer Emmy van Leersum (1930–1984), made a clean break from traditional jewelry. This diverse group of goldsmiths, designers, and sculptors used non-precious materials to establish a new form of jewelry that was independent of associations with wealth or traditional status.

Bakker had trained as a goldsmith at the Gerrit Rietveld Academie in Amsterdam from 1958 to 1962 but felt this instruction had only made him fit "to make expensive trinkets for rich elderly ladies," which he considered a poor goal for a life's work.[3] Van Leersum had attended the Institut voor Kunstnijverheisonderwijs in Amsterdam between 1958 and 1962 and then spent a year at the Konstfack Skolan in Stockholm. Together, Bakker and van Leersum sought to change deeply entrenched attitudes about jewelry by making it affordable to a socially varied public. Their underlying idea was that jewelry should promote equality. Rather than drawing inspiration from older Dutch jewelry makers such as Esther Swart-Hudig (b. 1924), Chris Steenbergen (b. 1920), and Riet Neerincx (b. 1925), Emmy van Leersum was inspired by contemporary painting and sculpture, which she saw at large exhibitions such as Documenta in Kassel, Germany, and in the museums of Paris and Amsterdam.[4]

Fig. 1 Gijs Bakker, *Neckpiece, 1967,* aluminum, Collection of the Museum Het Kruithuis, 's-Hertogenbosch, The Netherlands

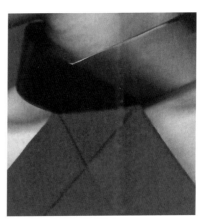

Fig. 2 Emmy van Leersum, *Collar with Fastening and Dress, 1968,* aluminum and textile, Collection of the Museum Het Kruithuis, 's-Hertogenbosch, The Netherlands

To shock the public out of its materialism and to encourage people to associate the jewelry they wore with artistic concepts and good design rather than monetary status, Bakker and van Leersum replaced precious metals and gemstones with aluminum, stainless steel, and rubber, often taken directly from industrial or domestic applications. The diversion of steel and aluminum from their original purposes to jewelry making recalled Marcel Duchamp's "Ready-Mades," which were such banal objects of everyday use as a bottle holder, a snow-shovel, or even a urinal, jarringly placed in exhibition settings normally associated with art objects. Just as Ready-Mades demonstrated Duchamp's disdain for the generally accepted concept of what constitutes art, Bakker's jewelry demonstrated his redefinition of jewelry.

Bakker and van Leersum focused on minimalist forms stripped of extraneous ornament, figuration, or historical references. Their eye-catching flamboyant works were no longer mere accessories to clothing. The body-oriented, industrial look that they championed became known as Dutch Smooth (*Hollands Glad*).[5] Some of their pieces, particularly their large, sculptural neck collars and head decorations (figs. 1 and 2), bordered on the theatrical.[6] Bakker relished using unmodified industrial materials and forms in imaginative creations such as his celebrated aluminum *Stovepipe Neckpiece and Bracelet* of 1967 (fig. 3). These large works required the use of lightweight materials, principally aluminum, and reflected the artists' ambitions to work as sculptors for the human body.

Fig. 3 Gijs Bakker, *Stovepipe Neckpiece and Bracelet, 1967,* aluminum, Collection of the Museum Het Kruithuis, 's-Hertogenbosch, The Netherlands

Van Leersum was not interested in the practical side of wearing jewelry; finding unusual ways to link function and form was what mattered to her. She used lightweight materials for her large works, but chose steel for her smaller jewelry, making weight itself an essential aspect of wearing her work.

On both small and large scales, Bakker and van Leersum designed for the human body, even tailor-making works for a specific individual's physical characteristics, such as the stainless steel and leather headpiece *Profile of Fritz Maierhofer* that Bakker made in 1974 (fig. 4). In a statement in 1975, Van Leersum said she was "now involved with the body, so I wanted to dismantle all the old conventions and start afresh. From the beginning, there is the human arm and it needs a covering. An arm has, roughly, the shape of a cylinder, so I took standard cylinders as my basic form."[7]

Fig.4 Gijs Bakker, *Profile of Fritz Maierhofer, 1974*, stainless steel and leather, Collection of the Museum Het Kruithuis, 's-Hertogenbosch, The Netherlands

By insisting that their work be considered "sculpture to wear," Bakker and van Leersum sought to have their pieces valued as art objects. Van Leersum stressed that her sculpture was to wear, yet she readily admitted, "No one who didn't like it or subscribe to its aim could ever wear it."[8] The ambiguity between the functional aspect of her work when it was worn and its autonomous existence independent of the body made the word *jewelry* problematic. Ralph Turner (b. 1936) invented the title *Sculpture to Wear* for the first exhibition of work by van Leersum in London's Ewan Philips Gallery in 1967. [9] Bakker and van Leersum used the term *Objects to Wear* as the title of a 1969 Smithsonian Institution exhibition of contemporary Dutch jewelry that opened in Eindhoven and later toured the United States. An anonymous reviewer for *Sculpture International* wrote of the show: "The work, by an imaginative and brilliantly gifted Dutch couple, Emmy van Leersum and Gijs Bakker, was far more daring and entertaining than that of British artists. As the title of the exhibition indicates, they are concerned with large sculptural forms rather than decorative minutiae. The most remarkable creations were in stainless steel and aluminum. These took the form of large scalloped bracelets to wear on the upper arm or on the knee, and shoulder or neckpieces—futuristic, science-fiction fantasies such as one might expect to find in the TV series 'The Avengers.'" [10]

The use of non-precious materials solved another very practical problem. Gold and silver were expensive for young artists without an established buying public, and using them in jewelry required a certifying mark in many European countries. Jewelry makers welcomed and encouraged the shift to non-precious materials, relishing the freedom to experiment without the risk of losing their own investment in expensive raw materials. [11]

The very visible and acquisitive younger generation that had aggressively turned its back on anything representing tradition provided a receptive audience for Bakker and van Leersum's new concepts. In 1967, Bakker and van Leersum dramatically displayed their jewelry in the groundbreaking *Sieraad III* (Jewelry III) show at Amsterdam's Stedelijk Museum. Instead of displaying their works on pedestals or showcases, they insisted on using live models to parade around wearing their new jewelry.

While Bakker and van Leersum's objects resembled manufactured goods on a cursory level, each was unique, skillfully crafted, and finished to achieve a "high tech" aesthetic. Bakker's beautifully formed *Bracelet* (1967) in the half-twisted form of a "moebius strip" (see no. 1) is an example of this artistry. The loop form, a common symbol of perpetual motion, appeared in many of Bakker's and van Leersum's works and reflected their interest in the Russian émigré sculptor and architect Naum Gabo (1890–1977), who completed his 26-meter-tall *Construction* monument in Rotterdam in 1957. Gabo's sculptural experiments with constructivism were often transparent geometric abstractions composed of plastics and other materials. [12] Bakker and van Leersum were also attracted to the work of the Swiss sculptor and architect Max Bill (1908–1994), whose constructivist outdoor sculpture in the 1950s was very popular. [13] Bill, who was the co-founder and director of the Hochschule für Gestaltung (School for Design) in Ulm, Germany (1931–1956), an important center for the dissemination of Bauhaus theories, was also influential in bridging the worlds of architecture and industrial design.

The contemporary Dutch painters and sculptors Ad Dekkers (1938–1974) and Peter Struycken (b. 1939), who focused on the abstract, geometric compositions of their works, were also sources for modernist geometric shapes that worked well with non-precious materials. In addition, the work of Dutch industrial designers such as Bruno Ninaber van Eyben (b. 1950) and the lamps and other products of Dutch architect/designer Aldo van den Nieuwelaar (b. 1944) also influenced the duo. The wearers of Bakker and van Leersum's minimalist forms were drawn into the artistic avant-garde with them, and creations by the two became powerful status symbols that were sought after by trend-setters.

Although they did not collaborate on individual pieces, Bakker and van Leersum created a body of between sixty-five and seventy works of jewelry that shared a common aesthetic. They used their first names, *Emmy* and *Gijs*, as their logos, and these became desirable status symbols much as designers' labels are today. While they valued their individuality, they exhibited well together and took advantage of the fact that duos were much in vogue.[14] It is ironic that despite Bakker and van Leersum's democratizing intentions and use of non-precious materials, their well designed, original, and elegantly finished pieces were expensive and were perceived as luxury commodities.

By the mid-1970s, Dutch Smooth dominated the jewelry scene in Holland. Other jewelers who adopted the same approach using non-precious materials included Nicolaas von Beek (b. 1938), Françoise van den Bosch (1944–1977), Hans Appenzeller (b. 1949), Lous Martin (b. 1945), Frans van Nieuwenborg (b. 1941), and Martijn Wegman (b. 1955). Appenzeller and Martin sought to lower economic obstacles to owning jewelry even further in order to encourage a change from wearing what one could afford, to wearing what one dared. In the spirit of creating jewelry for everyone, they opened the Galerie Sieraad in Amsterdam in 1969, focusing not on unique objects but on serially produced jewelry in such non-precious materials as Perspex, aluminum, and rubber. [15]

The influence of Dutch Smooth jewelry was so pervasive that the use of gold by the Dutch jeweler Robert Smit (b. 1941) was seen as shocking by his peers.[16] In the 1960s, Smit had made jewelry of acrylic and gold based on his own computerized drawings, but when he introduced works of gold alone in the 1980s, it ran counter to the Dutch Smooth trend and created an uproar. [17]

Whereas Bakker and van Leersum enjoyed considerable commercial success, it was government support that allowed Dutch jewelers in general great latitude to experiment. The high quality of the design and execution of the Dutch work led to a number of large-scale museum exhibitions in Holland from 1967 to 1970 that were supported by governmental funding in an effort to promote Dutch jewelry to a wider audience.[18] The Dutch government also had a policy of purchasing works for its museums in order to encourage the development of Dutch jewelry makers.

Freedom from commercial considerations may have been a double-edged sword for Dutch jewelry makers, however. On the one hand, it encouraged jewelers in the use of non-precious materials and experiments in production methods; on the other hand, government subsidies to stimulate jewelry artists to design jewelry for serial production led instead to uninspired works lacking the design, workmanship, and originality of one-of-a-kind pieces or those produced in limited series.

In a further effort to make their designs more generally available, Dutch jewelers began to produce work serially for sale in department stores. Despite the lower cost of these designs, or perhaps because of it, these works did not capture the imagination of the public. Too weak to stand out in the marketplace, they were perceived as akin to mass-produced costume jewelry. Nor were they taken seriously by collectors or museums, two important authorities on taste. These serially produced works had neither a one-of-a-kind aura nor a personal signature that could set them, and consequently their wearers, apart. [19]

THE NEW ELITE

Bakker's approach to creating jewelry of content, as opposed to jewelry of opulence, became increasingly rational and conceptual as the years progressed. In the same spirit in which the musician John Cage (1912–1992) removed emotional content from his compositions to create music based on chance, Bakker used logic and rationality to replace expressive and emotional content in jewelry. Any compositional elements that hinted at emotional content, including, for example, humor, were consciously eliminated in favor of minimalist design.

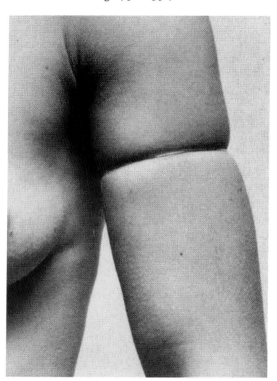

Fig. 5 Gijs Bakker, *Invisible Jewelry, 1975*,
skin mark, gold wire,
Courtesy of the artist

John Cage emphasized the importance of the act of performing to the musical experience, taking his concept to the limit when he directed concerts in which the musician sat at a piano but never played a note. Bakker made a similar statement in 1975 with his "invisible" jewelry, for which he directed that a gold wire be twisted tightly around the arm and then removed to reveal the imprint on the skin (fig. 5). The imprint became the jewelry, the ultimate form of non-preciousness through the dematerialization of the object, changing the body by performing an operation on it, and breaking with the notion of jewelry as enhancing beauty. Although Bakker exhibited the wire in a silk-cushioned box accompanied by a photograph of the imprint it left on skin, the lack of a tangible, wearable end product sparked a debate on the purpose of jewelry, the experiences of wearing and owning it, and the morality of materialism.

By subjecting the formal content of jewelry to a strict minimalist approach based on geometric logic, Bakker and van Leersum created an intellectualized, elitist style that appealed to a small audience of connoisseurs rather than to a wide public. Among the new jewelers, Bakker and van Leersum were philosophers who believed that "you could make design anonymous, that you could leave out the personal signature."[20] This approach caused considerable criticism and encouraged a counter-movement.

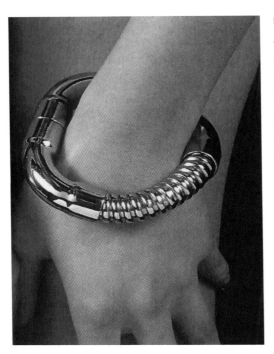

In 1968, a young Dutch jewelry artist, Marion Herbst (1944–1995), introduced work that contrasted with the anonymity of the minimalist works of Bakker and van Leersum.[21] In December of 1973 she formed the *Bond van Ontevreden Edelsmeden,* or BOE (*League of Rebellious Goldsmiths*), together with three other goldsmiths, Onno Boekhoudt (b. 1944), Françoise van den Bosch (1944–1977), Karel Niehorster (b. 1932), and the sculptor Berend Peter Hogen Esch (b. 1945). Although the BOE shared its disdain for the social prestige traditionally associated with jewelry, they offered playful resistance to the austere and dogmatic culture of the Dutch Smooth group, using non-precious materials with greater color, expressiveness, and humor. Herbst produced a successful series of

Fig. 6 Marion Herbst, *Bracelet*, 1971, chromed copper and shower hose, Collection of the Museum Het Kruithuis, 's-Hertogenbosch, The Netherlands

"shower hose bracelets," using flexible shower hose and elbow pieces as part of her drive to democratize her work with designs that were affordable for a wide public (fig. 6). In addition to aluminum and stainless steel, the BOE introduced more tactile materials such as papier-mâché and textiles with colorful embroidery. In many ways they were like post-minimal artists as they exploited the physical properties of soft and hard materials, matte and shiny surfaces, and mixtures of fiber and metal.

By the beginning of the 1980s, Dutch jewelry found itself at a crossroads between the prevailing rational/minimalist style and this emerging colorful, expressive work. It was during this period that British jewelry, long in the shadow of Continental jewelry, emerged to make a major impact in Holland.

As in Holland, youth in Britain became an important economic and social force soon after World War II.[22] The new youth culture in Britain first appeared in the 1950s, coinciding with the importation of early rock and roll from the United States, but expressing itself through a fashion subculture initially based on Edwardian styles (1903–1914), thus the "Teddy Boys" and "Teddy Girls." In the 1960s, another youth group, the Mods, descendants of the Teddies, appeared with a defiant "us-against-them" attitude. Generally poor, uneducated, and mired in low-paying jobs, they had a desire to share more fully in the new consumerism. They were fueled with the youth culture's rebellious spirit, and they became a major voice in determining new fashions in Britain.

One decade later, uneasy economic times in Great Britain were reflected in the Punk movement's harsh critique of authority. An outburst of bitterness and nihilism, Punk championed rebellious lifestyles and alternative fashions in much the same way that Hip Hop does today. An important aspect of Punk's broader impact on society was its expression of social, political, and sexual views through symbols of anger and aggression such as spikes and bullets, which were worn as inexpensive jewelry. Punk encouraged a sense of theater and flamboyance through body art, tattooing, piercing, and ripped clothes, showing that an individual could be political without being boring. During this period British designers became recognized leaders in international fashion.[23]

Although the proclivities of the younger Brits were at odds with what was considered educated taste, the new fashions had a profound impact on the art and culture of the period, notably British Pop Art, which dealt directly with fashion, innovation, and the consumer.[24] By linking fine art and popular culture, Pop Art had a democratizing element that was particularly strong in Britain.

Two prominent jewelers who appeared at this time were Wendy Ramshaw (b. 1940) and David Watkins (b. 1939), another husband and wife team. Ramshaw was educated as an industrial designer and had worked with non-precious materials. Watkins was originally trained as a sculptor and had been using acrylic for many years. Working together in 1964, Ramshaw and Watkins began designing black and white patterned acrylic pieces with the intention of making fashion jewelry based on the Op Art painting of the time.[25]

As David Watkins notes, "I was not involved in Pop Art, and didn't care for it as art, but it got into the bloodstream of the culture in a surprising way. I not only made sculpture, but also continued with music and became involved with fashion and jewellery in those years. I saw every experience as a creative opportunity. Everything was an adventure and anything seemed possible, and all these things have directly influenced my later work as a jewellery artist."[26]

Fig. 7 Wendy Ramshaw and David Watkins, *Optik Art Jewellery*, 1965, Perspex; *Something Special Jewellery*, 1967, paper, Collection of the Victoria and Albert Museum, London, United Kingdom

With less governmental support than their Dutch counterparts, British jewelers sought to be more aware of current fashions and commercial realities in order to seek out opportunities to show and sell their work. In 1965, Ramshaw and Watkins began their careers by forming the company Optik Art Jewellery. Their pieces, which were produced in quantity in an industrial process, were made by screen-printing special inks onto acrylic sheets. The individual pieces were then cut out, finished, assembled and packed (fig. 7).[27] Their work was designed to be ephemeral and favored the use of non-precious materials well before the new Dutch jewelry had appeared.

Although Optik Art failed when a large well-established fashion jewelry company made cheaper imitations of their designs using inferior materials, Ramshaw and Watkins went on to make other accessories and to participate in garment design for the trendy new "boutiques" in King's Road and Carnaby Street in London's West End. Ramshaw continued to make fashion jewelry in a variety of non-precious materials, including painted wood, wooden beads, and sequins.

27

In 1967, Ramshaw and Watkins formed the jewelry manufacturing company Something Special, which featured brilliantly colored paper jewelry that was sold in kits that were to be assembled by the wearer. Inexpensive and disposable, their paper jewelry incorporated such 1960s icons as Union Jacks, psychedelia, and Day Glo colors, and proved to be extremely popular as accessories with the paper clothes that were also fashionable. The couple were the first to produce and market paper jewelry that was well designed, and their idea was very much in the youthful spirit of the time.[28] Their jewelry received tremendous editorial promotion and was sold to department stores worldwide, including prestigious stores in Japan and the United States. At one point, the entire window of the Design Council in central London was devoted to their paper jewelry.[29]

When Watkins returned to jewelry after taking time out to design special effects models for Stanley Kubrick's film *2001: A Space Odyssey*, he observed that few of the developments in contemporary sculpture appeared in contemporary jewelry, with the exception of the work by the Pomodoro brothers Gio and Arnoldo (b.1930 and 1926, respectively) in Italy. In addition to their purely sculptural work, the Pomodoros created sculptural jewelry in large forms with strong textured surfaces that often reflected the influence of Abstract Expressionism. Watkins decided that jewelry could include the ideas he was pursuing in sculpture, and together he and Ramshaw set off on a course that opened up new directions for jewelry in Great Britain. The direction they decided on was encouraged in 1973 when they had their first exhibition in the United States and were introduced to collectors who were open to new ideas—of whom there were very few in Britain at the time. [30] The experience had a pivotal impact on Watkins, who maintained closer ties to the United States throughout the 1970s than to Europe. [31]

Both Watkins and Ramshaw produced jewelry that was markedly individualistic, often with figurative elements and unusual combinations of materials, in contrast to the stark Dutch Smooth productions. Watkins took a sculptural approach to his jewelry, using many materials not formerly used by jewelers, including titanium, gilded brass, colored and dyed acrylic, and neoprene (see no. 49). [32] His technically demanding neckpieces were made of colored acrylic rods that were inlaid with bands of metal and connected with precise hinges and joints or circles of fine steel wire and geometric attachments coated in colored neoprene (fig. 8).

Ramshaw became best known for her innovative combinations of rings that are displayed as sculptures on elaborate stands when not worn. Although Watkins and Ramshaw worked individually, their early jewelry was presented in joint exhibitions at Goldsmiths' Hall, Electrum Gallery, and the British Crafts Centre in 1974.

New jewelry in Britain developed in concert with clothing fashions, reflecting the vitality and inventiveness of the new clothing styles and the social statements they made. [33] The emergence of a new generation of artist-jewelers educated in art programs that had been established in the 1960s, together with a growing wealthy clientele who demanded less formal, more "modern" jewelry, hastened the process. As the role of jewelry as accessory was explored, the body became the foundation for wearable forms, with added importance given to the attitude of the wearer.

Fig. 8 David Watkins, *Neckpiece*, 1974, acrylic and silver, Collection of the Science Museum, London, United Kingdom

A vital area in which British jewelers distinguished themselves and took the initiative was in the use of fiber. One of the major pioneers in this experimentation was David Poston (b. 1945), who rejected the use of gold in large part because of the exploitation of black labor in South African gold mines. Poston worked with string, hemp, and cotton, as well as bone and leather, to produce works that not only were elegant, sensual, and economical but in their stand against apartheid represented a very contemporary and potent social statement by both artist and wearer (fig. 9). [34]

Fig. 9 David Poston, *Two Necklaces,* 1974–75, hemp, cotton, and silver, Collection of Mary La Trobe-Bateman and the British Crafts Council

One of the more important artists working with fiber during the 1970s was Caroline Broadhead (b. 1950), who from 1969 to 1972 had studied jewelry at the Central London School of Arts and Design, where visiting lecturers included Wendy Ramshaw, as well as Gijs Bakker and Emmy van Leersum. In order to create jewelry that had commercial possibilities, such as commissions for wedding rings, Broadhead chose to use silver and ivory in her early work, but she had broader interests related to the role of jewelry. [35]

Two events took place in the early 1970s that allowed Broadhead and other British jewelers to develop their work without having to make compromises in order to sell it. In 1971, the Electrum Gallery opened in London, the first to specialize in avant-garde jewelry. [36] It soon became the center for the newest developments in Britain and Europe, with exhibitions of works by Wendy Ramshaw and by Emmy van Leersum and Gijs Bakker. Through these exhibitions, the gallery fostered a British interest in jewelry as a viable art form.

Also in 1971, the Crafts Advisory Council (later the British Crafts Council) was established in London to promote new initiatives in British craft, including jewelry. When Broadhead set up a workshop with two former students fom the Central School, Nuala Jamison (b. 1948) and Julia Manheim (b. 1949), they received a grant from the Crafts Council that enabled them to launch their commercial venture. [37] As was the case in Holland, British government support through the Crafts Council sought to bring jewelry to a wider public. This was complemented by the role of independent galleries, such as Electrum, that sought out new talent and the latest innovations but had to walk a fine line between dependence on sales and the need to establish a position as authorities on taste and the avant-garde.

Performance art was another influence on jewelry in the late 1960s and early 1970s. In Britain, the performance artists Gilbert and George (Gilbert Proesch, b. 1943, and George Passmore, b. 1942) created "Living Sculpture," beginning in 1969, while Bruce McLean (b. 1944) performed "Installations for Various Parts of the Body." The sculptor Tony Cragg made several pieces in 1972 in which selected stones and other objects were placed on his body so that when he moved, the work ceased to exist. Works such as these, in which the body was integral to the art, had a bearing on the changing and ambiguous relationship between clothing and fashion in the work of a number of British jewelry artists.

In the late 1970s, Caroline Broadhead visited several countries in East Africa where she was impressed with the size, boldness, and color of the body ornament. The jewelry that she saw incorporated materials that ranged from traditional textiles to products of Western industry such as fragments of zippers and metal bottle caps, and it conveyed information about the wearer's position within society. This convinced her that jewelry could dominate, rather than accentuate, the body. When she returned to England, she no longer felt the need to make her jewelry comfortable or subliminal and decided to make the expression of her ideas take precedence over the practicalities of traditional jewelry.

Broadhead moved progressively away from "hard" jewelry to making tactile jewelry that conformed to the body, changing its form when worn.[38] She constructed inventive bracelets and necklaces made with tufted nylon threads held in wooden frames, sometimes encased in silver, as in the 1978 *Neckpiece* (see no. 3). These works combined elegance with functionality and were influential in removing the distinction between jewelry and clothing.[39] In an approach similar in spirit to van Leersum's, Broadhead united the geometry of the circle to the shape of the body, but used nylon tufts to soften the overall appearance. The tufts also reduced the size of the hole of the neckpiece so that it had an independent life as an art object when not being worn. Broadhead considered the experience of wearing the neckpiece to be its most important feature, wanting it to feel interesting as it was being put on and while it was being worn. [40]

The support of the Crafts Council allowed Broadhead to be less concerned about commercial considerations as her jewelry became increasingly larger and more theatrical. She followed a logical development from, for example, armpiece to sleeve to garment, and made shirts that were interesting formally (each sleeve is eight feet long) while being highly decorative and even sensual.

Another student at the Central School, Susanna Heron (b. 1949), also explored the borders between clothing, jewelry, and performance art, using painted papier-mâché, cotton, and nylon. Like van Leersum, Heron found the term *jewelry* inadequate to describe her work and invented the term *Wearable*.[41] In contrast to the starkness of the Dutch objects, Heron's abstract shapes incorporated color and light, perhaps revealing the influence of her father, the painter Patrick Heron (b. 1920). Her acrylic *Jubilee Neckpiece* 1977 (see no. 19), which appeared in three versions, resulted from her long-standing interest in the relationship of flat planes to the body, including how a flat circle could be wearable.[42]

Her *Wearable* of 1982 (see no. 20) had the appearance of a hat but was never worn on the head at all. Instead, it was pushed off the back of the head like a sun hat, with the ties knotted at the neck to hang down the front of the chest like a scarf. Although "wearability" was the criterion that governed the forms of Heron's Wearables, they were also designed to be hung on the wall, often alongside a photograph of the object being worn; photography was considered integral to the exhibited work. This made the "idea of wearing more potent, because you knew you really could wear them, and they really would work."[43]

By the late 1970s, a recognizable British style in jewelry had developed. It centered on a vigorous use of non-precious materials, especially textiles, and experimentation in color, transparency, movement, and interchangeability of components.[44] According to Electrum gallery co-founder Barbara Cartlidge, "the national talent for tolerating any eccentricity makes it quite hard to shock the British Establishment to any serious extent," so jewelry made out of non-precious materials was introduced without a ripple.[45]

CROSSCURRENTS

The excitement generated in galleries carried over to the British Crafts Council and to British museums, which drew on government subsidies to mount exhibitions of British jewelry that also traveled abroad. One such traveling show, *Fourways*, created by Broadhead, Heron, Jamison, and Manheim with the support of the Crafts Council, opened at the Victoria and Albert Museum in 1977 and traveled for three years, ending its tour in Holland at the Galerie Ra in Amsterdam.

Galerie Ra had opened in 1976 and quickly became the focal point and the main outlet for experimental European jewelry, featuring works by Broadhead, Manheim, and Heron alongside creations from Dutch jewelers. Exhibitions of British work such as *British Jewellers on Tour in Holland,* which opened in 1978 at the Van Reekummuseum in Apeldoorn, and *Fourways,* which was presented in 1980, helped reverse the direction of the Dutch-British influence. From 1978 to 1980, the Netherlands was overtaken as the main center of pioneering jewelry design by more extroverted, less doctrinaire forms from Britain. These works had a powerful effect on Dutch jewelry, boosting the reaction against Dutch Smooth that was being led by Marion Herbst, who was among the first to appreciate the British individuality.

Although Marion Herbst had worked with textiles, it was Mecky van den Brink (b. 1951) who first started to work with textiles for jewelry in the Netherlands, closely followed by Beppe Kessler (b. 1952). Another Dutch artist who responded positively to the idea of textiles in jewelry was Lam de Wolf (b. 1949), who embarked on a series of works that ignored the boundaries between body ornament, installation, and performance art. De Wolf, who had no formal jewelry training, had studied in the Textile Department of the Rietveld Academie from 1978 to 1981, and made little distinction between jewelry to be worn and objects to be viewed.

De Wolf also brought other influences directly to bear on the underlying concepts of her work, including those of Eva Hesse (1936–1970), the German/American minimalist painter and sculptor. To de Wolf, jewelry was not intended to add value to apparel but to take precedence over it. In the early 1980s, Lam de Wolf experimented with multi-strand necklaces of shredded, wound, or knotted fabric that could be worn over the shoulder to cascade down the back but could also serve as wall hangings (see no. 7). "I want my work to be a challenge, to wake people up, which is one way for a designer to function."[46]

The sentiment expressed in de Wolf's 1981 statement recalls the freshness and fervor brought to Dutch jewelry when it was first introduced in 1969, before it became more or less entrenched as the style of a new Establishment. Lam de Wolf's stated objective was to make a social statement that was "deliberately rebellious, anti-establishment and anti-capitalist," while still seeking to "appeal to the wearer."[47] Like her British counterparts, she enjoyed making "Wearable Objects" that were not designed to last forever, such as her *Neckpiece* (1981) (see no. 8).

As the 1980s unfolded, the British use of color, textiles, and moldable forms continued to change the direction of contemporary jewelry, heralding a period in which artists stretched the limits of materials and forms and pushed back the boundaries of what could be worn.[48] Whereas industrial materials such as aluminum and stainless steel had been popular in the 1970s, materials such as paper, textiles, wood, and iron were favored in the 1980s. The lines between jewelry and clothing blurred even further as both were subsumed under the category of body adornment.

This direction was furthered by Caroline Broadhead, whose experiments following her African experience were influential in transforming jewelry into designs meant to emphasize the personality of the maker and the owner. The exploratory nature of much of the work by Broadhead and Heron in the early 1980s led them increasingly further from existing jewelry forms such as necklaces, brooches, and bracelets, and pushed the limits of wearability.[49] Intentionally raising the issue of the role of sculptural objects for the body, Broadhead in 1983 created her renowned *Veil Collar* (see no. 5) of finger-woven monofilament, which was closer to the *idea* of clothing than to clothing itself.[50] While using clothing forms as the basis for these works, she resisted modifying them to make them commercially marketable because that would have destroyed their identity as unique objects.

Broadhead wanted to make pieces that were ambiguously placed between jewelry and clothing. Her interest was in exploring the very notion of wearability, leaving open the social or theatrical context in which her pieces might be worn. An excellent example of this approach is the *Armpiece 22 in 1* (1984) (see no. 4); when displayed off the body, it is not apparent that the work is wearable, yet it is easily compressed to wearable size and when worn emphasizes movement and transparency.

As their constructions of papier-mâché, cotton, nylon, and wire became increasingly removed from jewelry, Broadhead and Heron aligned themselves more with the world of fine art. Eventually they severed all links with the Crafts Council and stopped showing their work in craft shows. [51]

Julia Manheim was also interested in exploring the limits of wearability, as well as the use of alternative materials, including metals,

synthetics, textiles, and paper. Her *Cowl Collar* neckpiece (1983) transforms plastic tubing (see no. 28) into a sophisticated, if ephemeral piece. It was made as part of a collection of work that explored the boundaries of scale, projection, and angularity within wearable objects, and was shown in a solo exhibition, *Wire-Wear,* in 1983. The various plastics she used were chosen for their range of color and because their lightness allowed her to make very large objects that could still be worn. Her creations were also designed to be freestanding objects when not worn. Her *Purple Bracelet* of painted newspaper (1986) (see no. 29) is over eight inches in diameter and expands the scale of jewelry with respect to the human body. Apart from being a passionate recycler, Manheim chose newspapers because they could be manipulated into many shapes, affording her the opportunity to transform a throwaway into a richly textured and colored form. Once the enthusiasm for introducing new materials and colors began to proliferate, the clear distinction between the Dutch and British styles seemed to disappear as artists absorbed an eclectic international approach.

Fig. 10 Pierre Degen, *Personal Environment,* 1982, wood and string, whereabouts unknown

The Swiss-born jeweler Pierre Degen referred to his portable structures, or "personal environments," as jewelry despite their stronger relationship to ceremonial and performance art. Degen pushed the size limits of jewelry by attaching weather balloons to handmade ladders meant to be hoisted onto the wearer's shoulders (fig. 10). His performance-based objects represented an attempt to expand the definition of jewelry from ornamentation for the body itself to design for the space surrounding it. Degen's personal environments echoed the theater work of Bauhaus artist and stage designer Oskar Schlemmer (1888–1943), notably his 1927 *Slat Dance* (fig. 11), in which the dancers' arms and legs were physically extended into space using light wooden rods.

The emphasis had shifted decisively from ornamental jewelry to a form that was an amalgam of clothing, sculpture, and performance art. The interaction of Dutch and British ideas in the 1980s led to extreme examples of how far the definition of jewelry might stretch, and as the relationship of jewelry to clothing and sculpture was tested and extended, forms were tried for virtually every part of the human body. Whereas these works made a significant contribution toward changing the traditional concept of jewelry, they were caught between the elitism of fine art and the reduced sophistication of clothing fashions. [52]

These wearable and non-wearable objects influenced artists in Europe, the United States, and many other countries and represented an international avant-garde look. Landmark exhibitions such as *Cross Currents: Jewellery from Australia, Britain, Germany, and Holland* (1984), sponsored by the Crafts Board of Australia, the British Crafts Council, the German Goethe Institute, and the Dutch Prins Bernhard Fonds, well as *The Jewellery Project* (1983), organized by the British Crafts Council Gallery in London with the support of American collectors Susan and Malcolm Knapp, were meant to capture the spirit of what was hailed as a new form of jewelry. These exhibitions were supported by government subsidies, and the sale

Fig. 11 Oskar Schlemmer, *Stäbetanz, Szenephoto mit Manda v. Kreibig*, 1923, Collection of the Oskar Schlemmer Theatre Estate.

of objects was not a major consideration for the exhibitions or the artists. The government subsidies granted to jewelers in Holland and Britain afforded them the luxury of disregarding concerns for salability in order to focus on their individual proclivities rather than market factors.

Although government subsidies had a favorable effect on innovations in jewelry made of non-precious materials, there were also unexpected results. Jewelry, in the course of its twenty-year evolution toward autonomous art, had become unwearable "objects to wear." Although the ambition of many jewelry makers was to conceive body decoration as art, their works continued to be judged as jewelry and generated little interest beyond a small circle of fellow makers and connoisseurs.

In the words of Barbara Cartlidge, one of Electrum's founders, "While Electrum raised a lot of dust with challenging exhibitions, it failed to make the connections that might have turned spectators into clients."[53] In attempting to use non-precious materials, and make their jewelry accessible to a greater number of people, jewelers had, in fact, produced a different exclusivity that restricted those willing to wear their works. Whether a work is minimal or flamboyant, the wearer is central to its existence. The wearer interacts with these works and is responsible for the visual and social context in which they are seen. The idea that a piece of jewelry is not complete until it is worn takes an element of control away from the artist.

Developments in sculpture and performance art were in part a reflection of artists' desires to maintain artistic control over the realization and presentation of their ideas. By the mid-1980s, Broadhead and Heron recognized the contextual problem with the works they were creating and aligned themselves more clearly with sculptural expression. In 1986, Caroline Broadhead wrote, "The last 20 years [1966–1985] have nearly exhausted this exciting and important phase of questioning the fundamental nature of jewelry."[54] Heron, who had proved to be one of the most successful exponents of the British version of jewelry as miniature sculpture, eventually abandoned jewelry to work on sculpture and installation art.

ONE DOOR CLOSES

To many jewelers, the sculptural exploration of the boundaries of jewelry and clothing was a cul-de-sac,[55] albeit one marked by intense creative energy. Even if artists drifted far afield from making jewelry that would attract an audience beyond the small world of collectors, the period was one of great creativity and innovation. However, through works of large size, flamboyance, and increasingly exotic combinations of materials, jewelers engendered a reaction by the end of the 1980s that led to a return to jewelry that was wearable and more clearly related to ornament.

When the traditions of the goldsmith's art were revisited in the late 1980s, they were reinterpreted and transformed in highly innovative ways using both precious and non-precious materials. Jewelers emphasized the value of craftsmanship and inventive compositions and produced wearable forms rather than forms that wore the person.[56] But it was not a return to the earlier world in which precious materials dominated; Pandora's box had been opened and all materials were fair game for the jeweler.

The end is easily foretold,
When every blessed thing you hold
Is made of silver, or of gold,
You long for simple pewter.
When you have nothing else to wear,
But cloth of gold and satins rare,
For cloth of gold you cease to care–
Up goes the price of shoddy.

William S. Gilbert, "The Grand Inquisitor's Song"
The Gondoliers, Act II

ACKNOWLEDGMENTS

My appreciation goes to Derek Ostergard for his invaluable insights and suggestions while he was in the midst of several major projects. I am also extremely grateful to Gijs Bakker, David Watkins, Wendy Ramshaw, Marjan Unger, and Desmond Moneypenny for reviewing the text and providing important comments and information.

Notes

1   From earliest times, jewelry has been made from a wide range of materials, and frequently of combinations of precious and non-precious materials whose worth is highly variable as a function of time and culture. While material content alone may contribute to the monetary value, it is rarely the sole determining factor. The Vikings and Anglo-Saxons used iron and bronze, the Egyptians used colored glass and faience, and in eighteenth-century Berlin, iron jewelry was used as a political statement when gold and silver were needed to finance wars.

2   A thoughtful and insightful discussion of preciousness as content is found in Helen W. Drutt and Peter Dormer, *Jewelry of Our Time: Art, Ornament and Obsession* (New York: Rizzoli, 1995), pp. 76–80.

3   Barbara Cartlidge, *Twentieth-Century Jewelry* (New York: Harry N. Abrams, 1985), p. 112.

4   Antje von Graevenitz, "Communicating Mentalities: A Rhetoric of Dutch Jewelry 1950–2000," in *Jewels of Mind and Mentality: Dutch Jewelry Design 1950–2000* (Rotterdam: Het Kruithuis, Museum of Contemporary Art, 2000), p. 25.

5   The name was coined in 1968; "smooth" was also understood to mean impersonal and anonymous by those who objected to the dominance of the style.

6   Van Leersum's neckpieces are strongly related to the garment, sometimes with the dress literally hanging from the collar, whereas Bakker's neckpieces focus attention on the face. Bakker sought to make his neckpieces as large as possible without overwhelming the wearer.

7   As quoted in Cartlidge, *Twentieth-Century Jewelry*, p. 7.

8   "Algemeen Dagblad," January 24, 1970, as quoted in Yvonne G. J. M. Joris, ed. *Broken Lines: Emmy van Leersum 1930–1984* (The Hague: Gegevens Koninklijke Bibliotheek, 1993), p. 15.

9   von Graevenitz, "Communicating," p. 29.

10   *Sculpture International* 2 (1969): 19.

11   The Dutch jeweler and curator Riet Neerincx noted, "Looking back, I sometimes think that artists sought refuge in those other materials because they didn't need a maker's mark. Plus the fact that gold was expensive." As quoted in Jaap Huisman, "New Jewelry for a Renewed Country, 1950–2000," in Joris, *Broken Lines*, p. 82.

12   Together with his brother, Antoine Pevsner, Gabo wrote the *Realist Manifesto* (1920), which proposed that new concepts of time and space be incorporated into works of art and that dynamic form replace static mass.

13   Max Bill studied at the Arts and Crafts Academy in Zurich (1924–27) and was later a silversmith (1927–29) before studying at the Dessau Bauhaus.

14   Gijs Bakker, Communication with author, October 2001.

15   Huisman, *New Jewelry*, p. 52.

16   Clare Phillips, *Jewelry from Antiquity to the Present* (London: Thames and Hudson, 1996), p. 196.

17   Ralph Turner, *Jewelry in Europe and America: New Times, New Thinking* (London: Thames and Hudson, 1996), p. 32.

18   The venues included the Kapelhuis in Amersfoort, Galerie Nouvelles Images in The Hague, the Van Reekum Museum in Apeldoorn, and the Stedelijk Museum in Amsterdam.

19   Some jewelry from that period did achieve mass-market success, as in Frans van Nieuwenborg and Martijn Wegman's aluminum *Neck Zipper* and Bruno Ninaber van Eyben's *Pendant Watch*. Both were designed for manufacture and sold in much the same manner as Swatches— that is as novelties, rather than as objects created by an individual for an individual.

20   As quoted in Huisman, *New Jewelry*, p. 63.

21   Riet Neerincx stated: "What Herbst did was revolutionary. She threw a real spanner in the works," Huisman, *New Jewelry*, p. 55.

22   A strong ethnic component was incorporated into American music, making the music more intriguing in other countries, and creating a world idiom of popular culture. Mel Van Elteren, *Imagining America: Dutch Youth and Its Sense of Place*. (Tilburg, The Netherlands: Tilburg University Press, 1994), p. 9.

23   In 1965, Mary Quant's miniskirt appeared, and Chelsea became an international conglomerate of fashion, cosmetics, fabrics, and other consumer items, helping to make London a trend-setting capital.

24   The Pop Art philosophy was crystallized by Richard Hamilton, who is credited with heading the British Pop Art movement: "All art should be 'popular,' that is designed for a mass audience, transient, expendable (easily forgotten), low-cost, mass-produced, youthful, witty, sexy, gimmicky, glamorous, and big business." Susan Compton, *British Art in the 20th Century* (Munich: Prestel-Verlag, 1986), p. 192.

25   David Watkins, Draft essay for the Society of Jewellery Historians, September 2001.

26   Ibid.

27   Materials such as plastics, particularly Perspex and vinyl, were predominantly used in costume jewelry and by fashion designers, for example Paco Raban and Charles Jourdan.

28   Drutt and Dormer, *Jewelry of Our Time,* p. 112.

29   Their work appeared in many of the trend-setting clothing shops. The complete collection of original work from the mid-1960s, including prototypes, was purchased by the Victoria and Albert Museum.

30   The exhibition was undertaken with support and encouragement from Graham Hughes at the Goldsmiths' Company and from Helen Drutt in Philadelphia. Watkins, personal communication with the author, September 2001.

31   Watkins acknowledges the influence of Stanley Lechtzin, Olaf Skoogfors, Albert Paley, and Arline Fisch, personal communication with the author, September 2001.

32   The thin film of oxide that covers titanium can be transformed into a spectacular array of iridescent refracted colors when the metal is anodized. That effect began to be exploited in the 1970s by the British jeweler Edward de Large (b. 1943) in a series of brooches with futuristic and illusionistic perspectives.

33   Turner, *Jewelry in Europe and America,* p. 18.

34   Ibid. p. 66.

35   In 1974, Broadhead won the annual DeBeers competition with a gold and diamond bracelet, although the diamonds were camouflaged.

36   The founders of Electrum were Barbara Cartlidge, who had managed its precursor, the Pace Gallery, and Ralph Turner.

37   Before these two events, jewelers had to rely on editorials in fashion magazines such as *Honey, Vogue, Harpers,* and *Queen* to publicize their work.

38   Susanna Heron, "Britain," in Helge Larsen, ed., *Cross Currents: Jewelry from Australia, Britain, Germany, and Holland* (Sydney: Power House Museum, 1984), p. 33.

39   Turner, *Jewelry in Europe and America*, p. 64.

40   Caroline Broadhead, letter to Donna Schneier, August 2001.

41   Heron, "Britain," in Helge Larsen, ed. *Cross Currents,* p. 35.

42   Heron had discovered that a rigid circle could sit quite flat from the back of the neck, between the collar bone and shoulder, to the chest. Artist's statement, July 7, 2001. David Watkins had pursued similar studies several years earlier.

43   Artist's statement, July 7, 2001.

44   Cartlidge, *Twentieth-Century Jewelry*, p. 14.

45   Ibid.

46   Exhibition catalogue, *Objekt en Image*, 1983, as quoted in Evert Rodrigo, *Concepts, Comments, Process: Dutch Jewellery 1967–87* (Amsterdam: Rijksdienst Beeldende Kunst, 1987), p. 73.

47   Artist's statement, 2000.

48   In 1986, Marion Herbst's exhibition of papier-mâché works was presented at the Gallery Ra under the title *Irresponsible Design.*

49   In the late 1970s, Heron and the photographer David Ward worked together to produce a series of light projections designed to create patterns of light on the human figure.

50   In 1986, Broadhead was included in the show *Conceptual Clothing* at the Ikon Gallery in Birmingham. By 1989 she had moved full time into performance art. Tanya Harrod, *The Crafts in Britain in the 20th Century* (New Haven: Yale University Press, 1999), p. 429.

51   Harrod, *Crafts in Britain,* p. 428.

52   David Watkins remained essentially independent of the crossover between textiles and jewelry and continued to explore new materials and techniques within a minimalist aesthetic.

53   Barbara Cartlidge, *Celebrating Electrum's 25th Anniversary: The Innovators* (London: Electrum Gallery, 1996), p. 2.

54   Caroline Broadhead, *New Tradition: The Evolution of Jewellery 1966–1985* (London: British Crafts Centre, 1985), p. 7.

55   Fritz Falk and Cornelie Holzach, "Modern Jewellery" in *Schmuck der Moderne 1960–1998: Bestandskatalog der modernen Sammlung des Schmuckmuseums Pforzheim* (Stuttgart: Arnoldsche, 1999), p. 63.

56   Even Gijs Bakker began to use diamonds, albeit juxtaposed with everyday materials like laminated newspaper photographs of sporting figures.

Gijs Bakker born **1942**
Maintains a studio in Amsterdam, The Netherlands

"When someone wears a piece of jewelry, it becomes part of his body. Together with clothes, it gives him the possibility to show to other people who he or she is. We think that it is very important to work on this, to give people some clear alternative which helps them to discover themselves and helps them to show who they are."

(Donald J. Willcox, *Body Jewelry—International Perspectives* [Chicago: Henry Regnery Co., 1973], pp. 220–21.)

1

BRACELET, 1967
Aluminum
4 1/2 x 5 1/2 x 1 1/2 in.

Liv Blåvarp born **1956**
Maintains a studio in Skreia, Norway

"Non-precious material is a great artistic freedom. My thoughts and my work depend on a material such as wood. I like the beauty of the wood itself and the fact that I can work in an experimental fashion without fear of considerable waste."

2

BRACELET, 1987
Wood, elastic
4 x 4 1/2 in.

Caroline Broadhead born 1950
Maintains a studio in London, England

"Visiting Eastern Africa in the late seventies, I was impressed by the jewelry I saw—its size, abundance, color, and boldness. It was visually dominant and socially significant, carrying coherent information about the owner's place in society. Wearability, size, weight, and quantity were considerations for the jewelry maker and the wearer. In contrast, during my training, there seemed to be an assumption that jewelry had to be comfortable, sort of invisible, not to be experienced in a definite way. After observing African jewelry in context, Western jewelry seemed restrained and disempowered. It was at this point that I began to clarify my intentions in my work and the criteria by which I would judge it. The expression of ideas began to take precedence over the practicalities of traditional jewelry. I began creating pieces with two points of experience, one that was inside—wearing, feeling, handling—and one that was outside—viewing. I explored the tactile and the visual, the possibility of being both part of oneself and separate, subject and object. I also explored the way that pieces could be manipulated or changed."

3

NECKPIECE, 1978
Silver, wood, dyed nylon monofilament
8 in. (diameter)

4 **ARMPIECE 22 IN 1, 1984**
Cotton, nylon, monofilament
22 x 4 3/8 in.

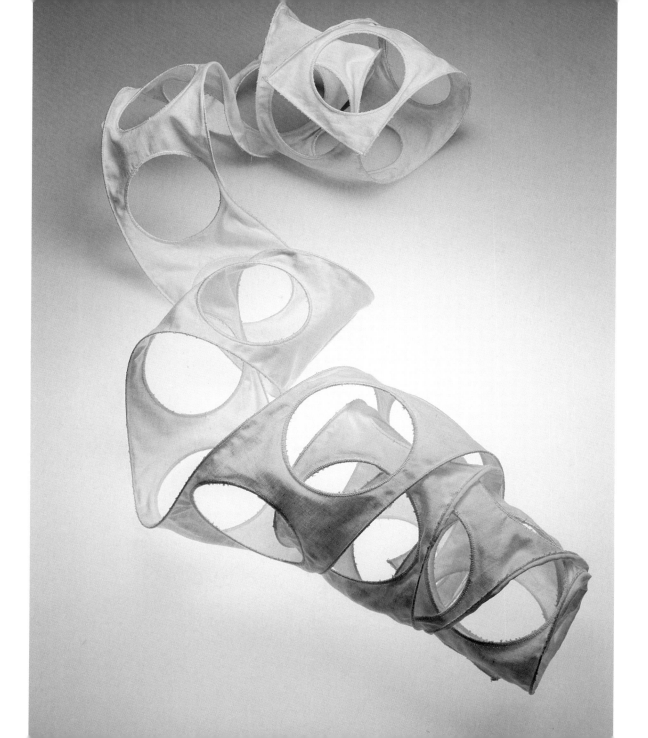

5   **VEIL COLLAR, 1982**
Monofilament, dye
11 1/2 x 1 3/4 in. (expandable)

Peter Chang born **1944**
Maintains a studio in Glasgow, Scotland

"To me, what is important is not whether a material is precious or non-precious but what its inherent qualities are. The plastics I use are mainly chosen for their range of colors and their malleability and finish. Plastics also have an anonymity that makes them a 'blank canvas' and invites me to make my mark."

6

EARRINGS, 1990
Acrylic, PVC, silver
2 1/4 x 1 5/8 in.

Lam de Wolf born **1949**
Maintains a studio in Amstelveen, The Netherlands

"Taking daily things out of their contexts, transforming them, and giving them new dimensions—so my work arises. In 1980 I introduced the term *wearable objects* for my work. With wearables, I wanted to make an artistic and social statement that was deliberately rebellious, anti-establishment, anti-capitalist. Wearables are exclusive and challenging; when you wear them, you know that you are being looked at, and you can feel your attitude changing. They are constructions for the body, but they could be hung on the wall or put on view somewhere."

7

**YELLOW SHOULDER
AND BODY PIECE, 1983**
Silk, paint
23 in. (length)

8

NECKPIECE, 1981
Wood, painted textiles
10 x 12 1/4 in.

Robert Ebendorf born **1938**
Maintains a studio in Greenville, North Carolina

"My conceptual approach to jewelry making explores alternative concepts and materials and also questions the nature of adornment itself. The creativity of my jewelry lies not simply in the intellectual repositioning of familiar objects but in more physical transformations of material that, in the end, challenge the viewer. And it is exactly this challenge that gives my pieces their beauty. It is the profound incongruity between what they are made from and what they are now that so engages the imagination."

9

FOLDED COLLAR, 1987
ColorCore, gold foil, Plexiglas, wood
12 in. (diameter)

10 **NECKPIECE, 1985**
Chinese newspaper, gold foil, hammered end caps,
ebony beads, rubber
14 x 10 x 2 in.

11

NECKLACE, 1986
Designed by Ivy Ross, b. 1955
ColorCore, wooden clothespins, rubber
12 1/4 in. (diameter)

Anne Finlay born 1953
Maintains a studio in Edinburgh, Scotland

"The early eighties was a time of change for jewelry designers in the U.K. and Europe. Traditional values were being questioned and through non-precious materials, jewelers began to move established boundaries. Before making these pieces in 1984, I had experimented with plastics, dyed aluminum, textiles, and painted wood, producing one-offs and several small series of variations on a theme. I found, however, that public perceptions were slow to accept and recognize that this type of jewelry could be 'precious' despite having little material value."

12

BRACELETS, 1984
Wood, paint, silk thread
3 x 2 1/2 in.

Arline Fisch born **1931**
Maintains a studio in San Diego, California

"Whether a material is non-precious or precious is not significant in my work, but I am drawn to color as an element, particularly strong color. In the machine-knitted work, it is achieved with copper wire coated with colored resins, while other pieces are fabricated in anodized aluminum, which can be dyed like fabric. The use of textile structures such as weaving, plaiting, and knitting enables me to produce pliable planes that conform to the human form and have a softness and warmth not always possible in metal. Each process has particular characteristics that affect the spirit and shape of a piece; each material contributes a different personality."

13   **CUFF (MKB67), 1985**
Machine-knitted coated copper, silver
21 x 6 in.

David Freda born **1953**
Maintains a studio in San Clemente, California

"Bird watching, taxidermy, falconry, scuba diving, and rock climbing have educated me to the point where I can express the natural world in an artistic sense. My forms are derived from these experiences. Some of my compositions feature realistic 'renderings' of animal forms while others are abstractions suggesting a particular theme. Often, I get an unexpected or surprising result by juxtaposing an animal image or abstraction rendered in twentieth-century materials such as aluminum, acrylic, or niobium with the sense of a natural habitat that is created via color, texture, and movement. I feel kinship with artists of the past whose intimate knowledge of the natural world also provided them with their concepts."

14   **VAGABOND BUTTERFLY FISH**
FROM HOOK, LINE, AND SINKER SERIES, 1985
Sterling silver, enamel, found objects
6 in. (diameter); 2 1/2 x 2 1/2 in. (fish)

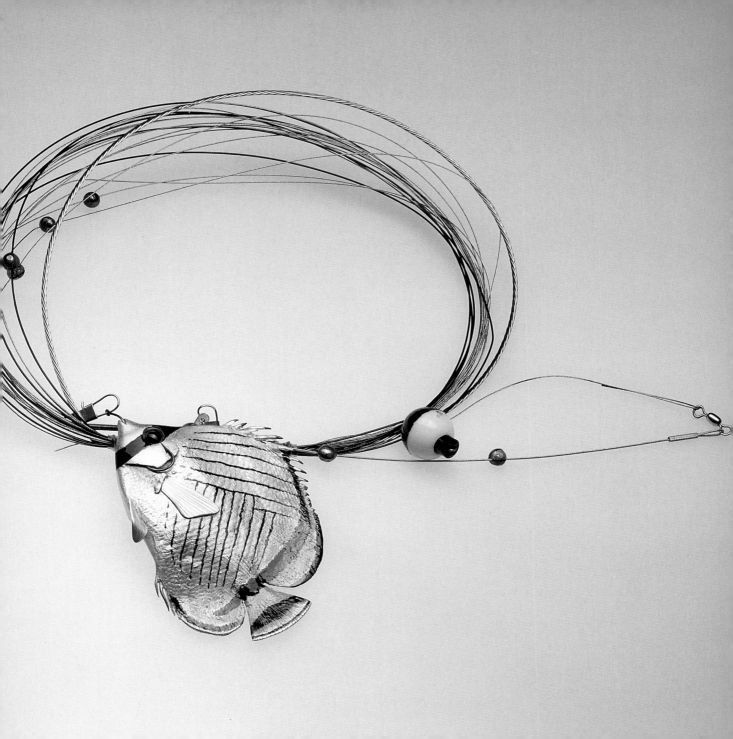

Douglas Eric Fuchs 1947–1986
Maintained a studio in New York, New York

"I'm not a purist. I don't use only natural materials. I've incorporated wire, plastics, paints and leather, as well as rolled papers in my work. The possibility of using whatever I want appeals to me. It leaves me a lot of room for trying things out in the future. It's reassuring to me. Someday I might decide to work exclusively in wire and plastics. I don't know, but I'd like to give myself the option."

(Douglas Fuchs, "Intrigued from the Start," *The Mercury*, May 3, 1982, p. 7.)

15   **NECKPIECE, CA. 1985**
Raffia
18 x 2 x 2 1/2 in.

Lisa Gralnick born 1956
Maintains a studio in Madison, Wisconsin

"In 1986, concurrent with my work in black acrylic, I enjoyed a modest yet sustained interest in theoretical physics, occasioned by serious study with several noted physicists and cosmologists, and I felt I had the beginnings of a very elementary understanding of the shared frontiers faced by twentieth-century artists and scientists. Artists have historically returned to issues of time, space, and the relativity with which we experience and interpret the natural world just as scientists, especially theorists, have. At the time, it seemed to me that many contemporary theoretical physicists were dealing with multidimensional concepts that were entertained nearly a hundred years earlier by the Post-Impressionists, Cubists, Surrealists, and Futurists. As the kinetic experiments I was conducting using rubber bands, paper clips, and coat hanger wire progressed, the frozen visual allusion of these black pieces seemed insubstantial, and this feeling ultimately motivated me to pursue a more direct, visceral involvement with an industrial aesthetic."

16

EARRINGS, 1986
Acrylic
2 1/4 in.

17

BROOCH, 1986
Acrylic
4 x 3 in.

Laurie Hall born 1944
Maintains a studio in Portland, Oregon

"In *Rah, Rah, Sis Bum Bah*, I was commenting on the preoccupation of society with sports, and also wanting an audience for 'art jewelry.' At the time, I was teaching art in a public high school in Mercer Island (Seattle), Washington, where the social agenda was driven by sports. I had a number of football players making necklaces in my jewelry class. At the end of the term they were all required to wear their necklaces around school for one day. It was all about getting attention for art's sake. I like sports and sometimes think they are everyman's art form. My neckpiece is more or less an announcement, or a 'sandwich board,' front and back, reporting on the action of the football game . . . the kick-off, the crowd, the goal posts, an evening of drama."

18   **RAH, RAH, SIS BUM BAH, 1985**
Copper, brass, plastic
19 x 6 in.

Susanna Heron born **1949**
Maintains a studio in London, England

"The three *Jubilee Neckpieces* that I made in 1977 for the Victoria and Albert Musem's Jubilee exhibition were based on my discovery that a rigid circle can sit quite flat from the back of the neck, between the collar bone and shoulder, to the chest. I wanted to see how wide I could make a flat circle without it becoming unwearable.

"My jewelry was always inspired by the activity of wearing. The material I used simply provided the means for making a piece that could not have been made in any other material without altering the work.

"My 'Wearables' were made in the image of those fashionable hats that you hang up and think about wearing, and try on in private, but rarely wear in public. These deceptively simple forms were remarkably evocative when worn. Wearing was both the function and the subject of these works."

76
77

19   **JUBILEE NECKPIECE, 1977**
Perspex, polyester resin
18 in. (diameter)

20

WEARABLE, 1982
Mutton cloth, wire
18 (diameter); 46 in. (ties)

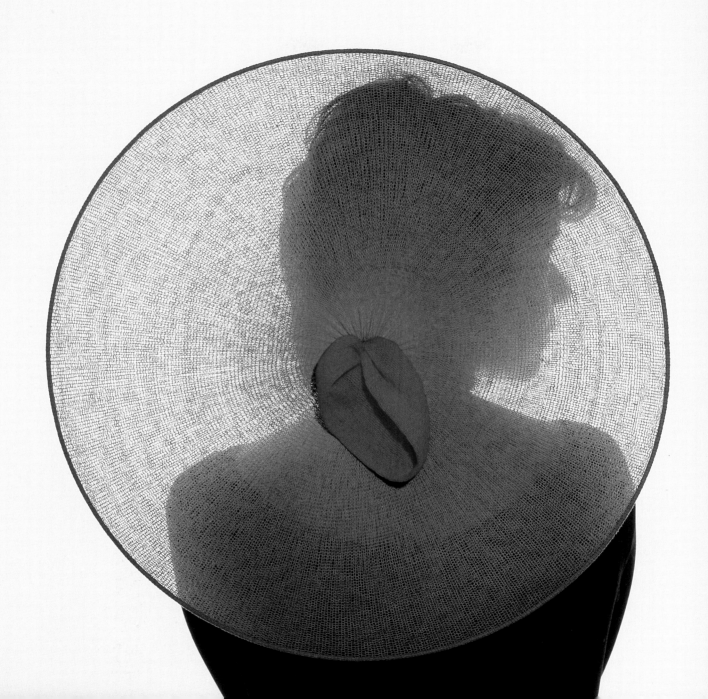

Esther Knobel born **1949**
Maintains a studio in Jerusalem, Israel

"I do not tend to 'explain' my work. I trust the viewer to do a good job. However, my work has always been about communication and dialogue. My choices of materials, techniques, scale, and image are means in the formation of content."

21   **CAMOUFLAGE NECKLACE, 1981–82**
Tin, fabric, paint,
15 in. (diameter)

22–24

#12 HOBEMAN, 1985
Tin, paint
6 x 6 in.

#13 ARCHER, 1985
Tin, paint
6 x 4 1/2 in.

#14 CRUSADER, 1985
Tin, paint
6 x 5 in.

Otto Künzli born **1948**
Maintains a studio in Munich, Germany

"In 1976 I was looking for fresh and uncommon ideas for jewelry as a new starting point in my work. I went several times to an instant photo booth and decorated my chest with steel wire, string, paper sheets, tapes, and paper dots. I was mainly interested in geometric shapes—dots, straight, curved or bent lines, circles, triangles, and squares, in both their two- and three-dimensional versions.

"In the following years I made several series of brooches based on this photographic research. I was interested in how far I could take the minimalization of geometric shapes as jewelry.

"After 1980, I used non-precious materials to express my ideas. A new ironic humor, as well as a new aggression, emerged in my work, resulting in creations such as *Ring for Two*, a piece that is self-explanatory."

25

NR 32040 BROOCH, 1982
Wallpaper, polystyrene
2 x 3 1/4 x 2 in.

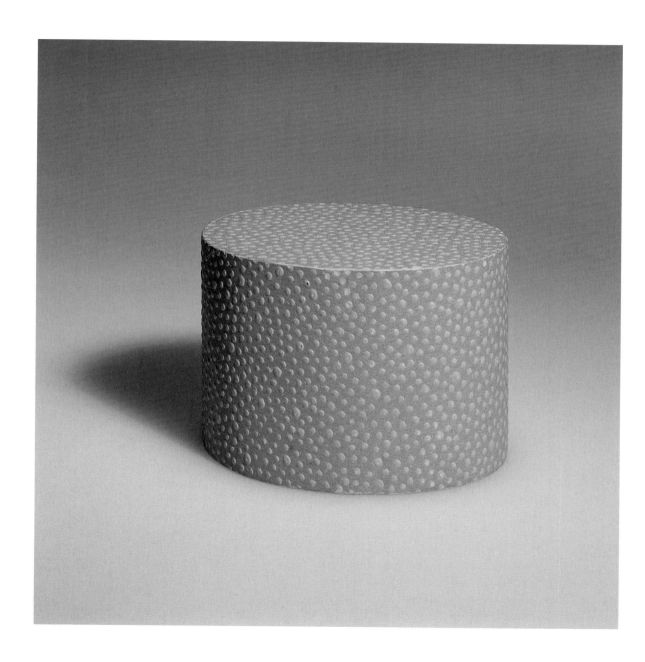

26   **RING FOR TWO, 1980**
Steel, silver, acrylic case
4 5/8 x 5/8 x 1/16 in. (ring)
2 3/4 x 6 3/4 x 3/4 in. (case, closed)

27   **GOLD MAKES YOU BLIND, 1980**
        Rubber, enclosed gold ball
        3 3/8 x 3 3/4 x 1/2 in.

Julia Manheim born 1949
Maintains a studio in London, England

The *Cowl Collar* was made as part of a collection of work that sought a more harmonious relation with the wearer. This was both a follow-up and a reaction to a previous body of work that explored the boundaries of scale, projection, and angularity. A variety of plastics were used for their range of color and because they were light enough to make something very large that could still be worn.

The *Purple Bracelet* is similar to jewelry and objects I was making at the time from newspaper, tearing and layering it in such a way that an exciting surface was created to paint on, and a mundane, throwaway material was transformed inro richly textured and colored objects. Apart from being a passionate advocate of recycling, I found newspaper appealing because it could be manipulated into any shape I required.

As a jeweler, I tried to explore and push limits, questioning the assumptions that people make about jewerly. There were forays into making multiples, too, but I always wanted to move forward and work on new ideas that required different materials and different ways of working. Making things that have never before existed and that have an uncertain outcome generates the excitement and desire to keep working.

28

COWL COLLAR, 1983
Plastic tubing
20 in. (diameter)

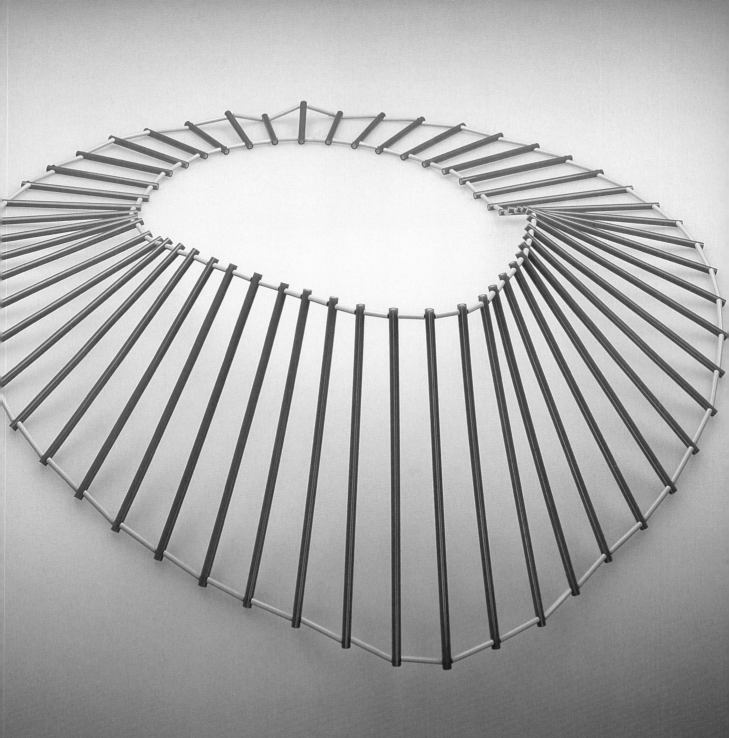

29   **PURPLE BRACELET, 1986**
Newspaper, paint
8 in. (diameter)

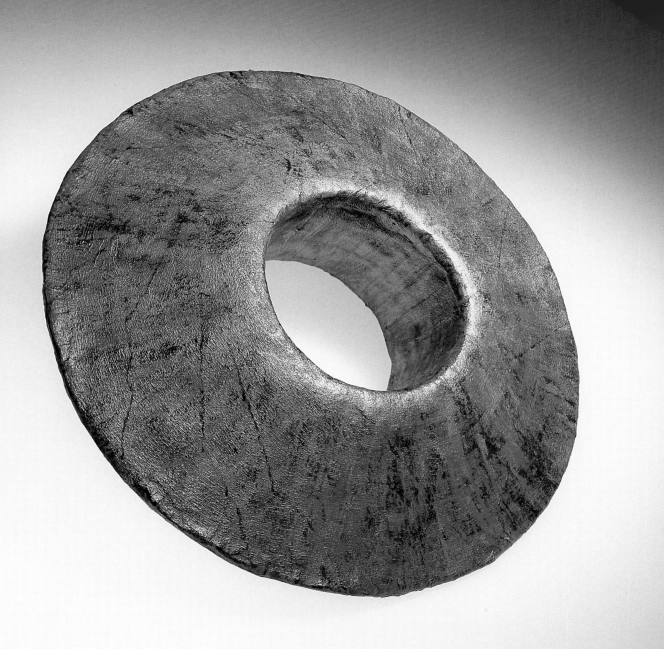

K. Lee Manuel born **1936**
Maintains a studio in Santa Cruz, California

"The highest art forms in many cultures are created for function as well as artistic statement. This has always had greater appeal to me than art that is made for walls only. Expressing that which flows through me has been the only motivation for my work.

"In the early 1980s, I returned from traveling in Japan with strong impressions of the culture and the imagery there. Imagination often fragments memory. *Shinto Shards* is made of some of the fragments of my memory, reassembled to create a kind of fairytale, or story. My main focus was on creating a painting, a wearable painting that would come alive and be experienced in movement."

30

SHINTO SHARDS, CA. 1987
Feathers, paint, multi-layered leather
17 in. (diameter)

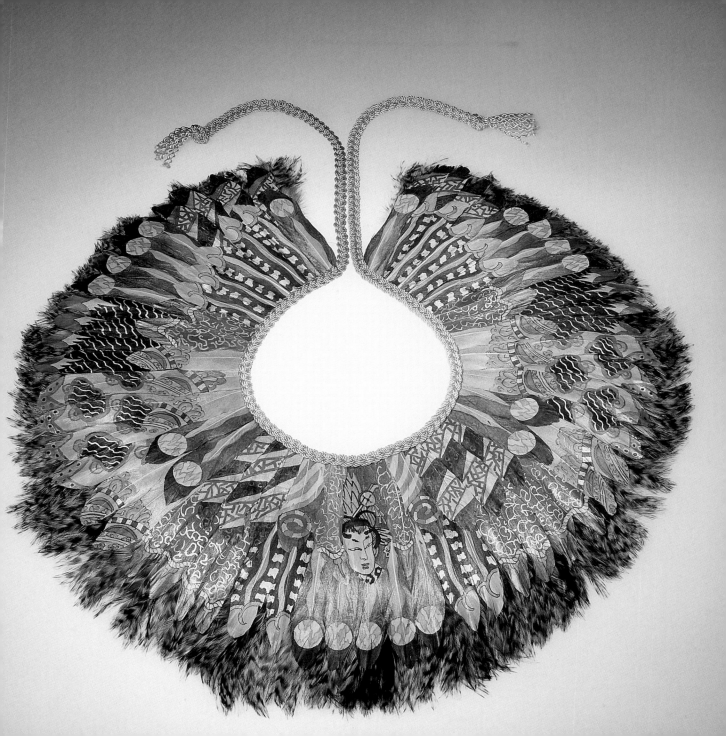

Wilhelm Tasso Mattar born **1946**
Maintains a studio in Artà, Mallorca, Spain

"At the time that I made this necklace, I was looking for a colorful material that would work as a substitute for enamel. My attitude was that of an explorer. I liked to work with precious and non-precious materials in combination. I was fascinated by the aesthetic of everyday material and relieved it of everyday life by making pretty things of it."

31   **COCA–COLA NIVEA NECKLACE, 1982**
Steel string, tin
9 1/2 in. (diameter)

Pavel Opočenský born **1954**
Maintains a studio in Prague, Czech Republic

"I have always been convinced that the preciousness of a piece of jewelry is the result of artistic understanding and accomplishment, regardless of the material. In 1986, my fascination ran toward fluid and organic form. A natural material such as ivory has a characteristic grain. My goal was to show and use this feature to its best artistic result. Mostly I created small sculptural objects that could be worn as brooches. Gradually the backside of the piece became more important in my overall concept. The weight of the brooch was really my only limitation."

32

BROOCH, 1986
Ivory
3 3/4 in. (diameter)

Rowena Park born 1959
Maintains a studio in Brighton, England

"I 'discovered' the principle by which this bracelet works when I was in college. I was interested in using non-precious materials and in exploiting their unique qualities. I was also searching for ways to express how a piece of jewelry like a bangle or bracelet encompasses a part of the body. I became aware of the properties of spring-tempered stainless-steel (used in dentistry for braces) by 'wrapping' lengths of the wire around my arm.

"At the time I was considering jewelry as art rather than pure adornment, although I was still conscious of the function of each piece that I made. I liked the fact that stainless-steel wire was not 'precious' and that a bracelet made of it would not be judged according to its intrinsic value in the way an item made from gold and diamonds would be. I felt, and still feel, that this is a purer concept since the wearer's only considerations are how the piece works and feels and looks. Price isn't important."

33   **BANGLE, 1982**
Spring-tempered stainless-steel wire, tubing
6 in. (diameter); 4 in. (depth)

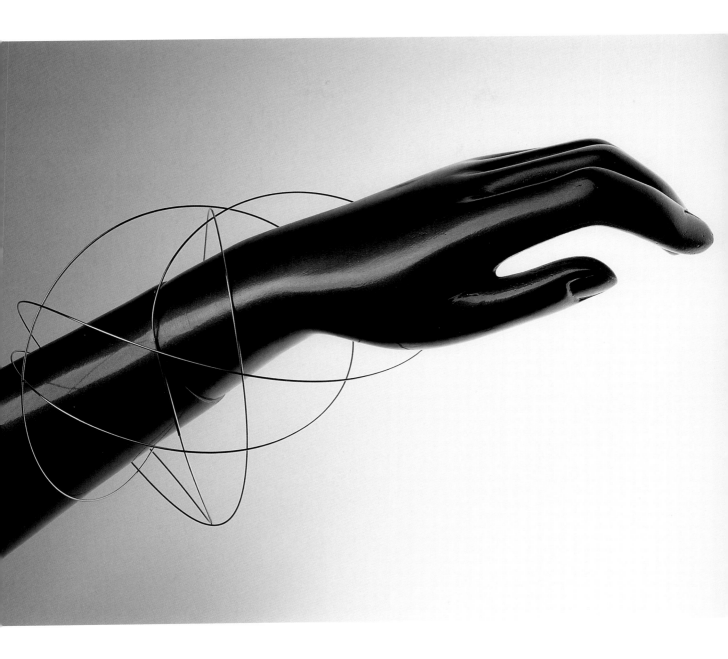

Michael Petry born **1960**
Maintains a studio in London, England

"The use of non-precious materials in my work stemmed from my performance art practice. In 1984, I formed the Media Arts Group to present site-specific performance work. The time-based nature of the performance pieces influenced my studio work and led me to experiment with paper-based objects. I intended that they be performance props as opposed to jewelry. However, they quickly became autonomous objects with titles that were intended to lead the wearers into role-playing situations in public spaces. It was less a rejection of precious materials than an outgrowth of work with paint in other media."

34   **THE MINOTAUR: HOMAGE TO PICASSO, 1984**
Paper, gold leaf, acrylic paint
Left to right: 16 x 19 1/2 in.; 4 1/2 x 5 1/2 in.; 14 1/2 x 17 in.

Hiroko Sato-Pijanowski born **1942**
Gene Pijanowski born **1938**
Maintain a studio in Honolulu, Hawaii

"In 1984, we began to work with Japanese paper cord, or *mizuhiki*, a traditional material developed over 250 years ago. Paper cord's strength in spite of its apparent fragility, and its threadlike form, are metaphors for life. The bright metallic colors of these paper cord pieces, traditionally associated with rituals of celebration, create an illusion of strength and permanence, an illusion similar to the one under which we live a large part of our lives. These colors, combined with exaggerated size and subtly erotic, contemporary forms, create a sense of drama and excitement."

35   **NECKPIECE AND BRACELET, 1987**
Paper cord (*mizuhiki*)
13 x 25 in.; 5 x 10 1/2 in.

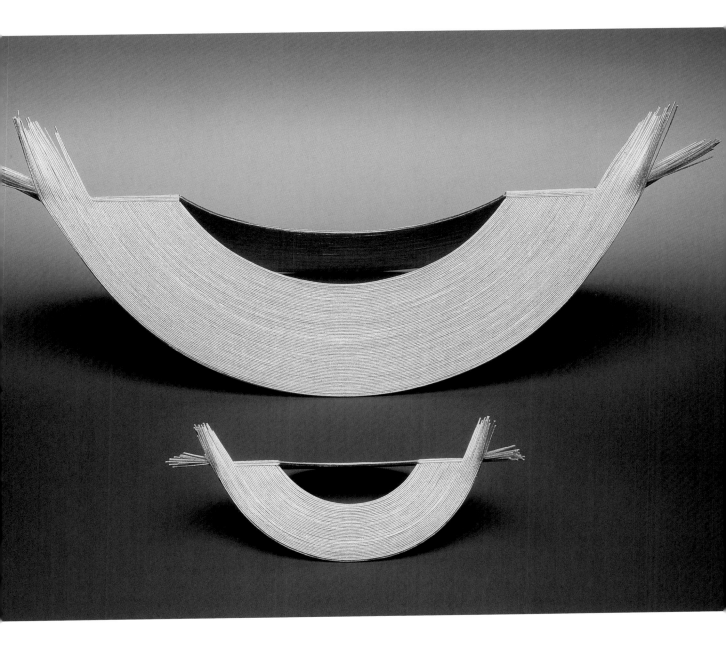

Wendy Ramshaw born **1939**
Maintains a studio in London, England

"All materials have their own special beauty. I hope my work can find a way to express and reveal that beauty. Ceramic is marvellous material to work with—exact form can be achieved with it. In many ways ceramic can be as beautiful as semi-precious stones.

"At the time of making the *Orbit Necklace* and *Orbit Earrings*, I saw no difference between working in precious and non-precious materials. The reason for using nickel alloy to make these pieces related entirely to its strength and color and to its suitability for the design. The only other appropriate material would have been stainless steel, but its hardness would have made it less sympathetic to the human form. This is not a statement about anything other than the design of the piece and the flexibility it offers to the wearer."

36　　　**WEDGWOOD PIN WITH CONE-SHAPED BEAD, 1982**
Blue and white jasper, brass
8 x 1 in.

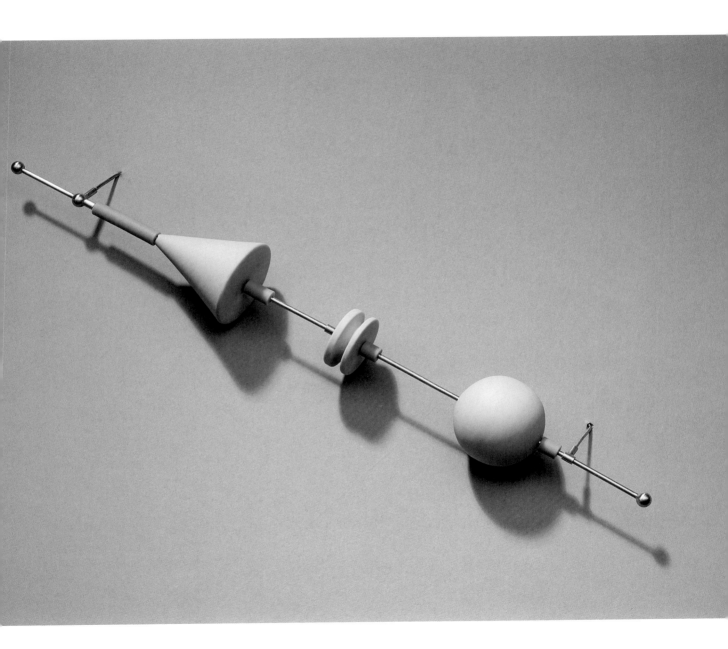

37   **ORBIT EARRINGS, 1988–89**
Nickel alloy, black resin
1 1/8 x 1/4 in.

38   **ORBIT NECKLACE, 1988–89**
Nickel alloy, black resin
9 1/2 in. (diameter)

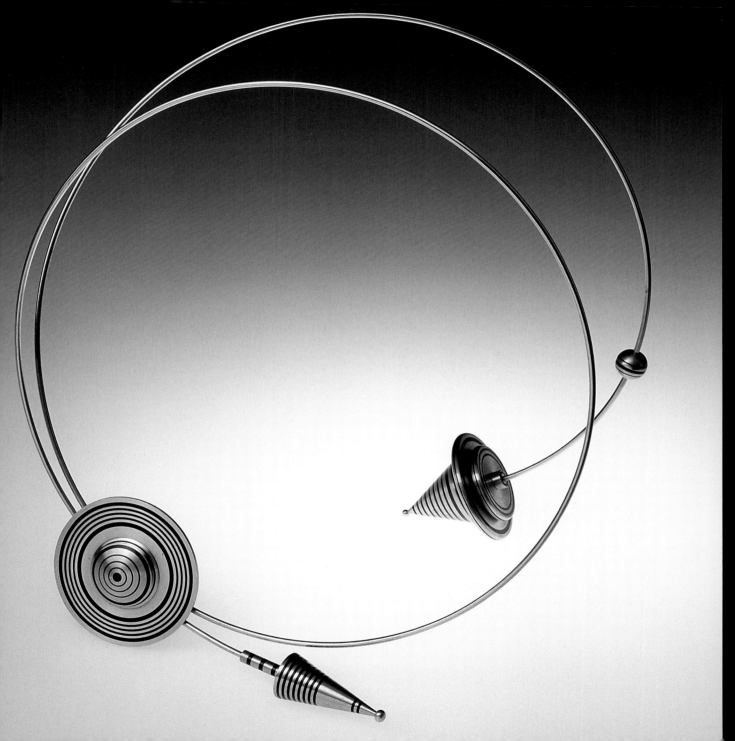

Vernon Reed born **1948**
Maintains a studio in Austin, Texas

"The creation of *Comet Zero* and my other cybernetic jewels resulted from my belief that cybernetics and microelectronics provided a natural (r)evolutionary path for jewelry in the late twentieth century. Just as the Etruscan goldsmiths worked at their culture's absolute technological horizon, I endeavored to make jewels appropriate for our age, utilizing on-board computers running custom software."

39   **COMET ZERO, 1985**
Plexiglas, battery, rubber, metal, LCD,
microcomputer, software
18 x 11 3/4 x 2 in. (overall)
9 x 6 x 5 in. (removable jewelry)

Marjorie Schick born **1941**
Maintains a studio in Pittsburg, Kansas

"Wearing a large, three-dimensional, colored drawing was intended to challenge both the wearer and the viewer. I have tried to stretch the idea of function in jewelry and have manipulated space by extending a brooch many inches beyond the wearer's shoulder or making a necklace so large that it nearly became a portable environment. Aesthetic concerns are of paramount importance, yet at the same time the work was meant to question the traditional boundaries of jewelry and to introduce theater and drama to body ornamentation. Each piece created is studied on the human body throughout its development to examine its relationship in terms of scale and shape to the wearer. These objects have a dual purpose: they adorn and glorify the body, and they have an existence as sculpture when they are hung on a wall or displayed on a pedestal."

40

BRACELET, 1987
Wood, rubber
6 1/2 x 8 1/2 in.

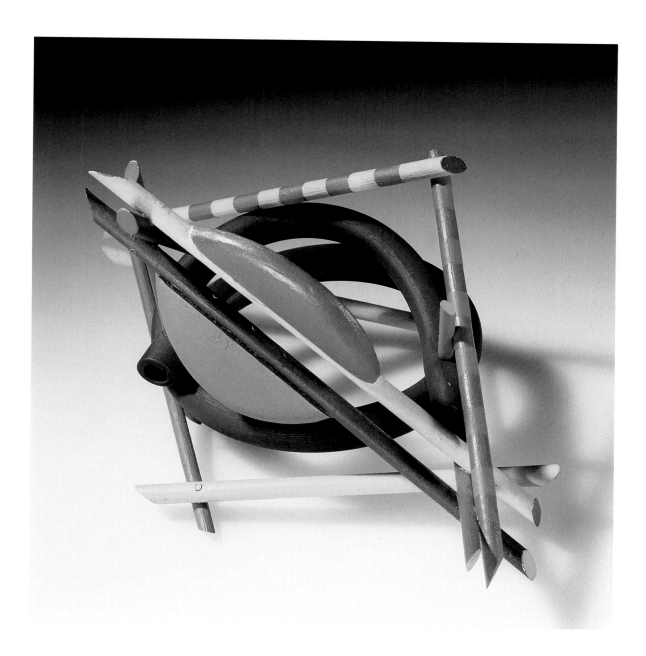

41   **BROOCH WITH TWO STICKPINS, 1987**
Wood, paint
18 x 4 1/2 in.

Verena Sieber-Fuchs born **1943**
Maintains a studio in Zurich, Switzerland

"I make jewelry, I put it in the world, and I let people react. My work is my language and my expression. I come from the field of textiles. Presently I work in two directions: textiles and jewelry. This is why I feel so free in making jewelry—and I enjoy it immensely. I do not want to be imprisoned in a certain category: I want to remain free and make that which gives me pleasure."

42

HEAD JEWELRY, 1986
Mickey Mouse paper
3 x 7 in.

43

APART-HEID, CA. 1988
Fruit-wrapping tissue paper, wire
16 in. (diameter)

44   **FIRECRACKER NECKLACE, 1986**
Firecrackers, wire, thread
21 1/2 (diameter)

Louise Slater 1956–1999
Maintained a studio in London, England

"Louise had a longstanding affair with the Orient, and particularly with the art and design of Thailand and Japan. Her parents lived in Bangkok for some years, and Louise spent a lot of time there.

"This necklace was from a collection of jewelry that reflected the influence of the Orient. The materials, although giving the appearance of natural products, are in fact manmade. They show how fine and delicate machine-made products can be."

(Communication from Louise Slater's husband, Victor Mann, January 2002.)

45

NECKLACE, 1985
Plastic, cablewire
12 x 6 1/2 in.

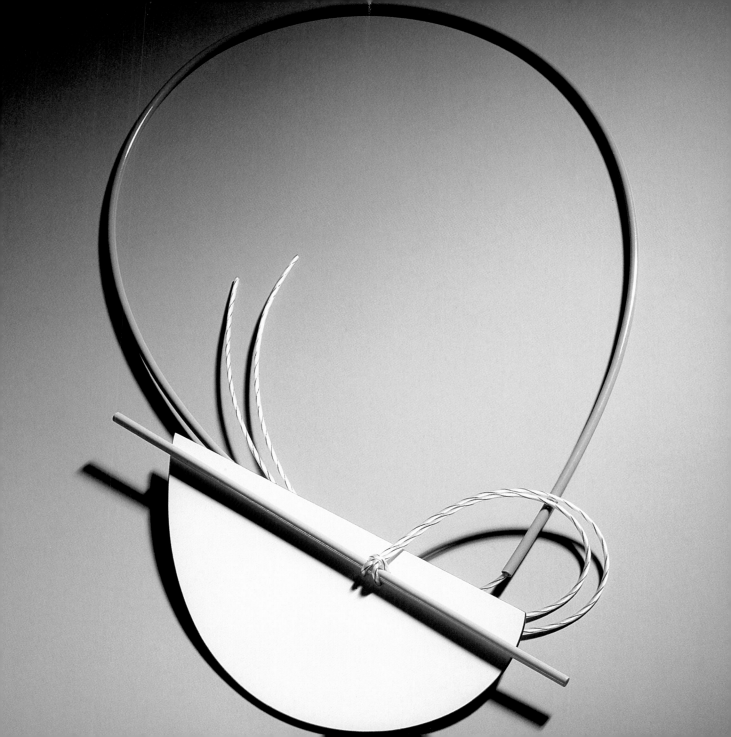

Emmy van Leersum   1930–1984
Maintained a studio in Amsterdam, The Netherlands

"Stainless steel is hard and stiff, it does not lose color or rust. For me it is better than silver. . . . I can cut it . . . into a steel tube and bend it . . . and it will stay in the new position without the need of solder."

(Ralph Turner, *Contemporary Jewelry: A Critical Assessment, 1945–1975* [New York: Van Nostrand Reinhold Company, 1976], p. 120.)

"I'm not sure that my work really has that much to do with jewellery. It's more to do with people, with shapes; getting away from simply buying gold. That tradition has never appealed to me. I think you should have a reason for wearing something."

("Amersfoortse Courant," *Veluws Dagblad,* December 12, 1979, as quoted in Yvonne G. J. M. Joris, ed., *Broken Lines: Emmy van Leersum, 1930–1984* [The Hague: Gegevens Koninklijke Bibliotheek, 1993.])

46

BRACELET, 1969–70
Steel
2 3/4 x 2 3/4 in.

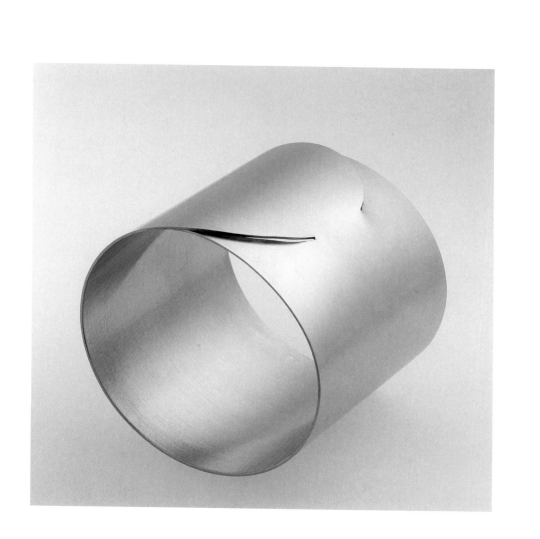

David Watkins born **1940**
Maintains a studio in London, England

"I have worked with a long-standing, self-imposed principle—rarely, and only very deliberately, broken— that my jewelry should express complete, autonomous forms, and that these forms should find their natural place on the body, without fastenings or other extraneous devices. For this reason, these works share the common, unambiguous, and generic frame of a circular neckpiece, needing only to be dropped over the head to complete their purpose. In this sense they are fundamentally 'primitive' and a 'statement' in themselves.

"I have no particular attitude toward non-precious or precious materials. I use materials that seem interesting, challenging, or appropriate to my ideas of the moment. I have always been more concerned with developing the form and meaning of jewelry than with the politics of its materials.

"I consider my work wearable. Demanding, maybe, but wearable. And beautiful. It seems obvious, but throughout my work I have been sustained by, or driven by, the singular vision of someone—whether an idealized abstraction or someone known to me—wearing each piece and, in so doing, transforming it. Without this, there would be no point."

47

TRANSFORMER #1, 1983
Paper
13 1/2 in. (diameter)

48

BARONG, 1983
Paper, wire
12 3/4 x 14 in. (4 parts)

49

VOYAGER, 1984–85
Wood, neoprene
13 1/2 x 13 in.

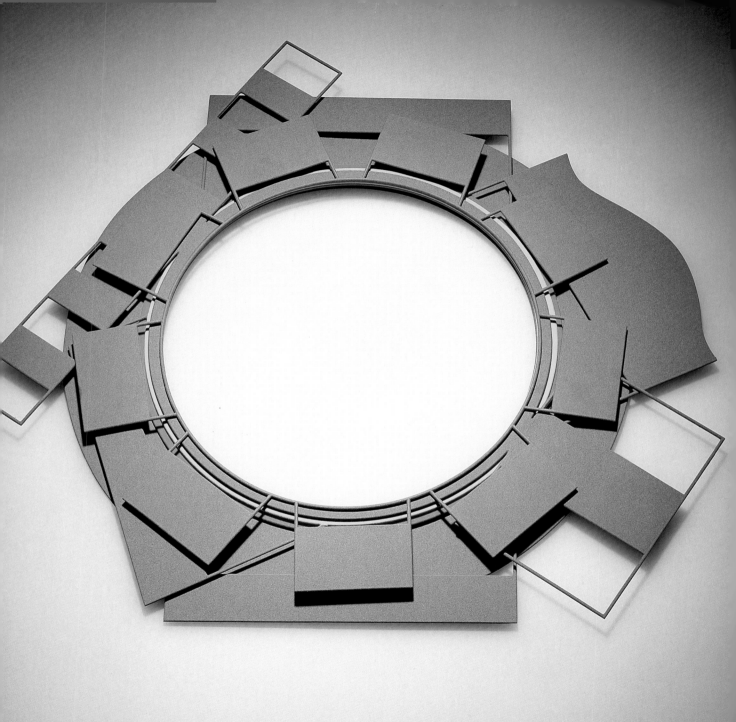

50

PAPER SPIRAL, 1983
Paper
10 3/4 in. (diameter)

Gijs Bakker

Born: 1942, Amersfoort, The Netherlands
Education: 1962, Konstfack Skolan, Stockholm, Sweden; 1958–1962, Gerrit Rietveld Academie, Amsterdam, The Netherlands
Current Residence: Amsterdam, The Netherlands

In the late 1960s, Gijs Bakker and his wife, Emmy van Leersum (1930–1984), helped to establish a new form of jewelry in Holland that was independent of associations with wealth or traditional status. Replacing precious metals and gemstones with aluminum, stainless steel, and rubber, often taken directly from industrial or domestic applications, Bakker and van Leersum created a minimal, industrial look known as Dutch Smooth that changed the course of the development of contemporary jewelry.

Bakker drew inspiration from contemporary sculpture and painting and also was strongly influenced by industrial design. In addition to jewelry, his work includes designs for home accessories, household appliances, furniture, interiors, public spaces, and exhibition spaces. Bakker has worked as a designer for numerous companies. Since 1987, he has been a professor at the Design Academy in Eindhoven, and in 1993, he co-founded the trend-setting company Droog Design, which had its debut that year at the International Furniture Fair in Milan. Among Bakker's numerous awards are the Françoise van den Bosch Prize in Amsterdam in 1988 and the Prince Bernhard Foundation Award for Applied Arts and Architecture in 1955.

Liv Blåvarp

Born: 1956, Furnes, Norway
Education: 1979–83, State College of Art and Design, Oslo; 1983–84, Royal College of Art, London
Current Residence: Skreia, Norway

Born in the countryside of eastern Norway, Liv Blåvarp creates jewelry that bears a close affinity to Norwegian folk art through her use of wood, a traditional material. She has extended traditional forms, however, with a contemporary sensibility and with innovative construction techniques that transform carved, laminated, and painted wood into flexible jewelry.

Blåvarp has made and exhibited jewelry continuously since the eighties, and her work has been shown throughout Europe, the United States, and Japan. In 1995, Blåvarp received the Thorsten and Wanja Soderberg Nordic Design Award for her original jewelry concepts.

Caroline Broadhead

Born: 1950, Leeds, England
Education: 1969–72, Central School of Art and Design, London; 1968–69, Leicester School of Art, England
Current residence: London, England

Caroline Broadhead began studying jewelry in London together with fellow student Julia Manheim just as non-precious materials were being introduced. Her visiting tutors included Wendy Ramshaw, Gijs Bakker, and Emmy van Leersum. Although Broadhead used silver and ivory in her early work, a visit to East Africa in the late 1970s encouraged her to create jewelry that conformed more directly to the body. Using tufted nylon and monofilaments, she created forms that combined elegance with functionality and in so doing she became one of Britain's most important modern jewelers.

Broadhead furthered the use of textiles and color in wearable ornament and was influential in reducing the distinction between jewelry and clothing. Her explorations of geometry and color led her to create work that was closely related to clothing—wearable in terms of comfort, fit, weight, and flexibility, but increasingly theatrical in context. By the mid-eighties, as she concentrated on the conceptual aspects of clothing and installation art, Broadhead's constructions had become increasingly removed from jewelry. In addition to receiving many awards and grants for her work in wearables, Broadhead was also honored with the prestigious Jerwood Prize for Applied Arts–Textiles in 1997.

Peter Chang

Born: 1944, London
Education: 1968–71, Slade School of Fine Art, University College, London; 1962–67, Liverpool College of Art
Current Residence: Glasgow, Scotland

Peter Chang was trained in graphics, sculpture, and printmaking. Soon after graduation from Liverpool College of Art, he went to Paris to study, where his interest in Surrealism was further heightened by lectures given by Marcel Duchamp, Man Ray, and Roland Penrose. Equally influenced by the bright colors and bold forms of Pop Art and his love of Chinese lacquer work, he combined all of these elements to create a fusion of East and West that reflects his British-Chinese ancestry—his father was Chinese and his mother, a fusion of Scottish, Welsh, and Italian.

Internationally recognized for his colorful and inventive forms, Chang began producing jewelry in 1984, working exclusively with plastic, a non-precious material he believes reflects the age in which we live. By 1988 he had had his first one-man show in Amsterdam. In recent years, in addition to his ongoing jewelry work, Chang has created furniture with elaborate, highly colored acrylic surfaces. He has also designed jewelry for fashion shows and collaborated with fashion designers, including the Turkish couturier Rifat Ozbek. Chang's awards include First Prize from the National Museum of Scotland in 1989, the Bursary from the Scottish Arts Council in 1994, the Jerwood Prize for the Applied Arts in 1995, the Inches Carr Trust Award in 1999, and the Creative Scotland Award in 2000.

Lam de Wolf

Born: 1949, Badhoevedrop, The Netherlands
Education: 1978–81, Gerrit Rietveld Academie, Amsterdam
Current Residence: Amstelveen, The Netherlands

Although Lam de Wolf's formal training was in textiles, she influenced the development of jewelry internationally in the 1980s. Disaffected with the minimalist Dutch Smooth style, she offered an alternative through a series of colorful, informal, and theatrical works that ignored the boundaries between body ornament, installation art, and performance art. De Wolf used shredded, wound, and knotted fabric, often painted in a bold variety of color combinations, that she toughened with glue and reinforced with rods to form a flexible whole. Asserting that jewelry should not add value to apparel but should take precedence over it, she created works that explored the boundaries between jewelry, clothing, installations, and wall pieces. In addition to exhibiting every year since 1982, de Wolf has taught at the Gerrit Rietveld Academie since 1985.

Robert Ebendorf

Born: 1938, Topeka, Kansas
Education: 1958–63, M.F.A. University of Kansas, Lawrence; 1954–58, B.F.A. University of Kansas, Lawrence
Current residence: Greenville, North Carolina

Robert Ebendorf is one of America's premier jewelry artists, celebrated for his imaginative combinations of materials. Ebendorf began his career in 1963 when he traveled to Norway on a Fulbright fellowship and was introduced to Scandinavian design concepts. He established himself as an innovative jeweler when he abandoned gemstones and precious metals for discarded remnants in the mid-sixties. His active curiosity has led to the pioneering inclusion in his work of a wide variety of materials, ranging from Chinese newspapers to natural river stones, Formica, and discarded consumer goods.

Robert Ebendorf has been an influential professor for over forty years. He taught at the State University of New York at New Paltz from 1971 to 1989 and currently holds an appointment as Belk Distinguished Professor at the East Carolina University of Art in Greenville, North Carolina. He is a Fellow of the American Crafts Council and a past president and Distinguished Member of the Society of North American Goldsmiths.

Anne Finlay

Born: 1953, Wick, Scotland
Education: 1971–76, Gray's School of Art, Aberdeen, Scotland
Current Residence: Edinburgh, Scotland

After studying jewelry making and weaving, Anne Finlay settled on jewelry as the artistic medium in which she would express herself, and she soon became known for her work in plastic, a material she chose for its wide range of colors, clean finish, and ease of use. In addition to acrylic and PVC, she has incorporated nylon, laminates, rubber, stainless-steel wire, textiles, and aluminum into her jewelry concepts.

Unlike many jewelers who chose non-precious materials as a statement against the social status implied by precious gems and metals, Finlay based her decision solely on aesthetic grounds. In recent years, she has turned her attention to timepieces, for which she has received major commissions, such as the painted steel clock she made for the South Edinburgh government offices. In 1984, Anne Finlay jointly won the Paul Reilly Prize at the Chelsea Crafts Fair, currently sponsored by the British Crafts Council.

Arline Fisch

Born: August 21, 1931, Brooklyn, New York
Education: 1966–67, Apprentice School for Gold- and Silversmiths, Copenhagen, Denmark; 1959, Haystack Mountain School of Crafts, Liberty, Maine; 1956–57, Kunsthaanduaerkerskolen, Copenhagen, Denmark; 1952–54, University of Illinois, Urbana-Champaign; 1948–52, Skidmore College, Saratoga Springs, New York
Current Residence: San Diego, California

Over her forty-year career, Arline Fisch has been a leading figure in studio jewelry. She pioneered the application of such textile techniques as weaving, knitting, crocheting, and braiding to metal to give it the flexibility of cloth. Using her knitted metals, she has created large, sensuous, sculptural jewelry that blurs the boundary between jewelry and clothing.

Arline Fisch is Professor Emeritus at San Diego State University, where she founded the school's jewelry program in 1961. She has exerted a strong influence on the development of contemporary jewelry through her exhibitions, her teaching, and her seminal book *Textile Techniques in Metal for Jewelers, Sculptors, and Textile Artists,* first published in 1975.

Her numerous outstanding honors include four Fulbright fellowships (in 1956, 1957, 1966, and 1967), four National Endowment for the Arts fellowships (in 1974–75, 1977, 1979, and 1981), and a Lifetime Achievement Award from the National Museum of Women in the Arts in 1994. Fisch was declared a Living Treasure of California in 1985. She was a founding member of the Society of North American Goldsmiths, and president of that organization from 1982 through 1985. A Fellow of the American Craft Council since 1979, she was awarded its prestigious Gold Medal for Consummate Craftsmanship in 2001.

David Freda

Born: 1953, Milwaukee, Wisconsin
Education: 1980–83, State University of New York, New Paltz; 1974–77, B.F.A. University of Wisconsin, Whitewater
Current Residence: San Clemente, California

David Freda began his artistic career as a wildlife illustrator, an occupation that grew out of his childhood interest in insects, reptiles, and other fauna. After taking a jewelry course out of practical necessity—he was flying birds of prey and needed to make bells to tie to their feet—he began his career as a metalsmith.

Influenced by the work of metalsmith Marsha Lewis, Freda spent a year as an artist in residence at the Oregon School of Arts and Crafts and then moved to New Paltz, New York, where he began graduate studies in metalwork. He now creates intricate enameled jewelry that incorporates his love and respect for the creatures of the natural world.

Douglas Eric Fuchs

Born: 1947, Yonkers, New York
Died: 1986
Education: 1976, M.A. Columbia University Teachers College (Art Education); 1975, Varpapuu School of Weaving, Varpapuu, Finland; 1966–70, B.A. Catholic University

After earning his bachelor of arts degree, Douglas Fuchs lived and worked with the aboriginal people of Australia, during which time he developed insight into the use of non-precious materials and basket-weaving techniques for body ornaments. Fuchs's jewelry emphasizes texture, color, surface decoration, myth, and ritual. In 1981, Fuchs received fellowships from both the National Endowment for the Arts and the Australian Crafts Council. Before his tragic death in 1986, Fuchs shared his knowledge and insights while working as a basketry instructor in the New York City public schools and at the New School for Social Research in New York City.

Lisa Gralnick

Born: 1956, New York, New York
Education: 1978–80, M.F.A. State University of New York, New Paltz; 1973–77,
B.F.A. Kent State University, Ohio
Current Residence: Madison, Wisconsin

A student of Kurt Matzdorf and Robert Ebendorf at the State University of New York at New Paltz, Lisa Gralnick explored the use of numerous materials, including precious metals, in her jewelry. Gralnick sought to create a perfect harmony between technology and art through her jewelry and was drawn to the precision and logical thinking required by metalsmithing.

In the 1980s, Gralnick became internationally known for her starkly geometric black acrylic jewelry that was suggestive of ominous missiles or submarines. Although she returned to working in precious metals in the 1990s, Gralnick remained fascinated by industrial mechanisms and created a series of pendants and neckpieces that included spools, pulleys, and other mechanical devices.

Her most recent work in gold utilizes paper models as inspiration to create lightweight, folded pieces that suggest temporality in a material that is normally associated with immortality.

In 1991, Gralnick became head of the metals department at the Parsons School of Design in New York City, a position she held for eleven years. She is now a professor in the art department at the University of Wisconsin–Madison. She was the recipient of a Louis Comfort Tiffany Foundation Grant in 1993, fellowships from the National Endowment for the Arts in 1988 and 1992, and four fellowships from the New York Foundation for the Arts.

Laurie J. Hall

Born: 1944, Portland, Oregon
Education: 1974–76, M.A.T. University of Washington, Seattle; 1962–66, B.A.
Willamette University, Salem, Oregon
Current Residence: Portland, Oregon

Laurie Hall is a descendant of an Oregon pioneer and instills the spirit of America in her jewelry. Encouraged by the jewelry artist Ramona Solberg, who taught at the University of Washington, she has used non-precious materials and found objects such as beads, button, bone, and game pieces in her work.

In the early 1980s, Hall introduced a strong narrative element into her jewelry, incorporating incidents from her life. Her jewelry took a more theatrical turn in the 1980s, often including a narrative that extended over the shoulders and onto the back. After thirty-five years of teaching, she is now working on her jewelry full time.

Susanna Heron

Born: 1949, Welwyn Garden City, England
Education: 1969–71, Central School of Art and Design, London; 1967–68, Falmouth School of Art, Cornwall
Current Residence: London, England

Susanna Heron first combined resin with silver in her jewelry in 1970 at the Central School of Art. As a student she was inspired by the film of Oskar Schlemmer's *Slat Dance* and his definition of "ambulant space," the three-dimensional space articulated by the body's movement. The live body and the personal activity of wearing were to become her primary concerns. Heron continued her exploration of materials in 1976, using acrylic to create a series of works that grew out of her longstanding interest in the spatial relationship of flat forms to the body. By 1981, finding the term *jewelry* inadequate to describe her work, she invented the term *Wearable*. Wearing was both the function and the subject of these works, which were exhibited hanging on the wall with photographs showing how they were to be worn.

Heron proved to be one of the most successful British exponents of jewelry as sculpture. In 1983, as Heron's constructions became increasingly removed from jewelry, she abandoned this art form to work on sculpture, and she now works internationally on site-specific projects, often collaborating with architects. In 1977, Heron was awarded a United Kingdom/United States Bicentennial Arts Fellowship to travel and work in the United States for one year. Since 1985 she has won numerous awards for her sculpture, including the Art for Architecture Awards from the Royal Society of Arts in 1996 and 1999, and a fellowship from the Arts Foundation in 2001. She was made an Honorary Fellow of the Royal Institute of British Architects in 1999.

Esther Knobel

Born: 1949, Poland
Education: 1975–77, Royal College of Art, London; 1970–74, Bezalel Academy of Art and Design, Jerusalem; 1968–69, Plastic Art Institute, Bat-Yam, Israel
Current Residence: Jerusalem, Israel

Following her studies in painting, Esther Knobel switched her concentration to jewelry, studying in Europe in the late 1970s during a time of great activity and innovation. Knobel returned to Israel in 1979, occasionally producing pieces that resembled weaponry and expressed her views on the political climate in Israel. More generally she has created colorful figurative objects that come alive fully only when worn. The warrior figures for which she is best known are constructed from used tin cans that she flattens, cuts out, and then colors or embosses.

Since 1981, Knobel has taught at schools in Israel and Europe and continues to exhibit her work throughout Europe and the United States. In 1986, Knobel won the Alix de Rothschild Foundation Prize for Jewellery, and in 1994, the Françoise van den Bosch Prize in Amsterdam. In 1996, she received second prize in the International Judaica Competition, and in 2000, the Jewelry Prize from the Ministry of Education.

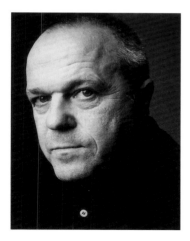

Otto Künzli

Born: 1948, Zurich, Switzerland
Education: 1972–78, Akademie der Bildenden Künste, Munich; 1965–70, Schule für Gestaltung, Zurich
Current Residence: Munich, Germany

Born in Switzerland and trained as a goldsmith in Munich, Germany, Otto Künzli is one of the most provocative and influential jewelers of the post-War era. A student of the renowned German jeweler Hermann Jünger, Künzli eventually succeeded Jünger as director of the goldsmith department at the Akademie der Bildenden Künste, Munich, where he continues to teach.

Since the 1980s, Künzli has brilliantly used his creations to question jewelry's traditional and contemporary roles. By raising the value of concept above the value of materials in a wide range of controversial and often seminal works, he exposed the blind acceptance of jewelry conventions. With highly accomplished craftsmanship, powerful imagery, and a sharp sense of humor, Künzli stands as a leading spokesman for contemporary jewelry. Künzli received the Françoise van den Bosch Prize in Amsterdam in 1990 and was made an Honorary Fellow of the Bezalel Academy in Jerusalem, Israel, in 1992.

K. Lee Manuel

Born: 1936, Loma Linda, California
Education: 1956–59, B.F.A. San Francisco Art Institute; 1954– 56, University of California, Los Angeles
Current Residence: Santa Cruz, California

From the time she began college, K. Lee Manuel was drawn to art. She became interested in making wearable art when she visited a museum warehouse and was appalled that so little art saw the light of day. Determined to make art a part of everyday life, she began painting garments for her growing family.

Manuel is perhaps best known for the garments she creates, some of which incorporate thousands of feathers and are evocative of clothing used in ceremonies in non-Western cultures. Although conceived as three-dimensional paintings that take account of the movement of the body, these extraordinary creations are often displayed off the body as well. Her richly complex pieces are sought by collectors and connoisseurs, including Diana Ross, Elton John, Barbara Rockefeller, and fashion designer Mary McFadden. K. Lee Manuel received a grant from the National Endowment for the Arts in 1988.

Julia Manheim

Born: 1949, London, England
Education: 1968–69, Hormsey College of Art, England; 1969–72, Central School of Art and Design, London
Current Residence: London, England

Julia Manheim studied in London with fellow student Caroline Broadhead when the use of non-precious materials in jewelry was being introduced. Following her graduation, she worked in silver and enamel and showed her work with Susanna Heron, Broadhead, and Nuala Jamison in the influential *Fourways* exhibition in 1977. By the early 1980s, Manheim had become interested in exploring the limits of wearability and in overturning notions of preciousness in jewelry through the use of alternative materials, including steel wire, plastics, and newspaper.

Julia Manheim's career has been marked by changes in direction from jewelry to sculpture to installation art. In 1991, Manheim received an exhibition grant from Greater London Arts, and in 1997, she was appointed principal consulting artist for Norden Farm Centre for the Arts, Maidenhead. She continues to live in London, working from a converted milk depot.

Wilhelm Tasso Mattar

Born: 1946, Schlangen, Germany
Education: 1974–79 Fachhochschule für Gestaltung, Pforzheim, Germany; 1969–74, University of Cologne, Germany
Current Residence: Artà, Mallorca, Spain

German-born, Wilhelm Mattar studied jewelry at the prestigious Fachhochschule für Gestaltung, Pforzheim. His jewelry has often carried political content, combining both figurative and abstract elements that reflect the influence of the 1970s Punk rebellion against authority and conformity. His work in the early 1980s included weapon-like ear pieces that were meant to be displayed on toy soldiers and were suggestive of a brutality that many found disquieting in jewelry.

Since 1979, Mattar has operated his Galerie Mattar in Cologne, Germany, which became noted for its support of avant-garde movements in contemporary jewelry. Mattar's current work still utilizes symbols drawn from contemporary society, such as Coca-Cola bottle caps transformed into colorful necklaces and brooches. In 2000, Mattar received the Amber Award from the Amber Association in Gdansk, Poland.

Pavel Opočenský

Born: 1954, Karlovy Vary, Czechoslovakia
Education: 1973–74, School for Jewelry and Metals, Turnov, Czechoslovakia; 1971–72, School for Jewelry Design, Jablonec nad Nisou, Czechoslovakia
Current Residence: Prague, Czech Republic

The Czech jeweler Pavel Opočenský started his career at the age of fifteen, during a yearlong apprenticeship in a metal workshop. Because of the repressive government in Czechoslovakia, following his studies, Opočenský often had to design jewelry covertly at personal risk, working mainly in wood and brass because of restrictions on access to gold. In 1979, he decided to leave his country, and he came to the United States in 1982, after spending three years in Germany.

In the United States, Opočenský took a job carving ivory and quickly realized its potential as a medium for jewelry. Residing in Brooklyn, his jewelry consisted of geometric pieces that reflected the jarring angularity of the New York cityscape. He turned to sculpting stone as well as such synthetics as ColorCore and Surell in response to political and environmental concerns over the exploitation of ivory. Opočenský returned to the Czech Republic in 1990, and since that time his jewelry has been exhibited frequently in Europe and the United States. Opočenský also works as a sculptor, and his sculpture has been shown recently in New York City and at the Long House Reserve in East Hampton, New York. He received a fellowship from the New York Foundation for the Arts in 1985 and a grant from the Empire State Craft Alliance in 1990.

Rowena Park

Born: 1959, Harpenden, England
Education: 1979–82, B.A. Brighton Polytechnic, England; 1977–79, Eastbourne College of Art and Design, England
Current Residence: Brighton, England

While at college in England in the late 1970s, Rowena Park became interested in using non-precious materials so that her jewelry would be judged on its artistic value rather than on the value of its constituents. Concerned with how jewelry feels and looks, Park chose to work with acrylics because of their lightness, color, pattern, and texture. She also used stainless-steel wire—identical to that used by orthodontists—to make bracelets that wrap around the arm.

The content of Park's work has changed in recent years, following trips to India, where she was overwhelmed by the vibrancy of colors, and New York City, where she was fascinated by the lines and scale of the urban landscape. She renders many of her impressions in clear acrylic that she hand paints with transparent glazes, gold leaf, and lacquer. Rowena Park continues to work from her studio in Brighton, England.

Michael Petry

Born: 1960, El Paso, Texas
Education: 1999, London Guildhall University; 1977–81, B.A. Rice University, Houston, Texas
Current Residence: London, England

Soon after graduating from college in Houston, Texas, in 1981, Michael Petry rolled a pair of dice in Las Vegas and wound up in London three days later. He co-founded the Media Arts Group to bring together live performance with visual art. In 1984, he assembled the exhibition *Movements in Jewellery* at the Electrum and Aspects galleries in London, featuring his own work as well as that of David Watkins and Wendy Ramshaw. A multimedia performance at Goldsmiths' Hall in London was choreographed in conjunction with the exhibition. Paper is Petry's preferred medium for jewelry, and his interest in adornment extends to painted clothing and headpieces. He has recently made a new body of work on the im/purity of pearls.

Michael Petry is best known as a world leader in installation art, but he has also made contributions to the field of performance art, writing the libretto and directing the opera *An Englishman, an Irishman, and a Frenchman*, with music by Gavin Greenaway and John Powell. He co-founded the Museum of Installation in London in 1990 and continues as its co-director.

Hiroko Sato-Pijanowski

Born: 1942, Tokyo, Japan
Education: 1966–68, Cranbrook Academy of Art, Bloomfield Hills, Michigan; 1965–66, California State University, Northridge; 1960–64, Rikkyo University (St. Paul's) Tokyo, Japan
Current Residence: Honolulu, Hawaii

Gene Pijanowski

Born: 1938, Detroit, Michigan
Education: 1967–69, Cranbrook Academy of Art, Bloomfield Hills, Michigan; 1959–67, Wayne State University, Detroit, Michigan
Current Residence: Honolulu, Hawaii

As classmates in metalsmithing at Cranbrook, Hiroko Sato and Gene Pijanowski met and married, beginning a creative partnership that has lasted to this day. The goal of their collaboration has been to apply advanced technical methods to alter the appearance of metals until they are transformed into visual poems, whether seen on or off the body.

The Pijanowskis studied traditional Japanese techniques for altering the surface color and texture of metals in order to figure out how to create the illusion of soft fabric and natural organic patterns in their own metalwork. They have also investigated the properties of non-precious materials, notably *mizuhiki*, or paper cord, a traditional Japanese decorative material in use for over 250 years. Currently they are designing and creating jewelry with CAD/CAM software. The Pijanowskis imbue all of their jewelry with a depth of thought and richness of feeling that reflects the contemplative nature of Zen philosophy.

The Pijanowskis are widely collected and have been honored with numerous international awards. In 1987, they received the prestigious Herbert Hoffmann Prize at the Internationale Handwerks Messe in Munich. In 2000, they became Fellows of the American Craft Council.

Wendy Ramshaw

Born: May 26, 1939, Sunderland, England
Education: 1956–60, Newcastle-upon Tyne College of Art and Industrial Design, England; 1960–61, Reading University, England; 1969, post-graduate studies, Central School of Art and Design, London
Current Residence: London, England

Although she was trained as a designer of printed textiles and an illustrator, Wendy Ramshaw has played a major role since the early 1970s in establishing British jewelry as an international force. Coming from a background in design, she was free from the fetters of jewelry traditions, and has been successful for over thirty years. Ramshaw is best known for her innovative combinations of rings, which, when not being worn, are meant to be displayed on elaborate stands, as sculptural objects.

Widely traveled as a visiting artist, Ramshaw has absorbed many influences and incorporated many materials into her work, ranging from feathers to ceramics and glass. The acrylic and paper jewelry that Ramshaw designed with her husband, David Watkins, in the 1960s has been preserved in the archives of the Victoria and Albert Museum.

The Worshipful Company of Goldsmiths elected Ramshaw as Freeman of the Company and named her a Lady Liveryman in 1986. In 1993 she was awarded the Order of the British Empire for her services to the Arts. Ramshaw is a Fellow of the Royal Society of Arts and an Honorary Fellow of the London Institute. In 1999 she was elected Royal Designer for industry.

Vernon Reed

Born: 1946, Pine Bluff, Arkansas
Education: 1996–98, M.A., Radio, TV, Film, University of Texas, Austin; 1967–71, B.A., Psychology, University of Texas, Austin
Current Residence: Austin, Texas

After studying psychology as an undergraduate, Vernon Reed took a metalsmithing class in the 1970s and then went on to teach himself to work in gold, using both lost-wax casting techniques and forging techniques. He then moved on to electroformed jewelry, in the first of what would be a series of investigations using advanced technology to produce jewelry. In 1975, Reed became the first person to make LCD electronic jewelry, and in 1985 the first to make cybernetic jewels with on-board computers. His wearable computers and his cybernetic artworks have been shown in major museums in the United States, Europe, and Asia.

Reed returned to school in 1996 to obtain a master's degree in radio, television, and film and has now become a self-titled "new media interactivist" specializing in the exploration of virtual reality systems. His current interest is in Avatar Virtual Worlds, which are computer-generated digital spaces that are accessed over the Internet.

Marjorie Schick

Born: 1941, Taylorville, Illinois
Education: 1983, Sir John Cass School of Art, City of London Polytechnic, London; 1963–66, M.F.A. Indiana University, Bloomington; 1959–63, B.S. University of Wisconsin, Madison
Current Residence: Pittsburg, Kansas

Marjorie Schick has had a major impact on the field of jewelry since the late 1960s when she created sculptural papier-mâché forms and linear "drawings to wear" inspired by the sculpture of David Smith. Schick earned an international reputation in the 1980s with her sculptural "stick" forms that related colors to the shapes and rhythms of the human form and the immediate space around the wearer. In the spirit of constructivism, with a suggestion of Pop Art, she used slender colorful dowels to delineate negative space in a series of easily recognizable works.

In recent years, Schick has introduced plywood and canvas into her work, and her painted surfaces have become more complex, with built-up layers of color and texture. She continues to teach and work at Pittsburg State University in Kansas. In 1990, Schick was awarded the Distinguished Alumni Award from Indiana University School of Fine Arts, Bloomington. In 2000, Schick was made a Fellow of the American Craft Council.

Verena Sieber-Fuchs

Born: 1943, Appenzell, Switzerland
Education: 1965–69, Kunstgewerbeschule, Basel and Zurich
Current Residence: Zurich, Switzerland

Verena Sieber-Fuchs initially worked with textiles on a monumental scale, creating tapestries and textile installations for the interiors of large public buildings. In 1973, she began to make jewelry using traditional materials, including glass and metal beads, which she crocheted into cords and collars. In 1983, she began to incorporate light and transparent materials such as tissue paper and gossamer filaments into her jewelry, making it airy and spacious. This new approach introduced novel effects to the structure, rhythm, color, and, especially, form of her designs.

Sieber-Fuchs continues to create non-traditional jewelry by painstakingly stitching together materials such as paper, metal wire, and, often, discarded items that add provocative non-jewelry associations that range from the humorous to the deeply political. Sieber-Fuchs received First Prize at the Sixth International Jewelry Exhibition in Tokyo, Japan, in 1986 and was awarded the Prix Michelin et Jean Jacques Brunschwig in Geneva, Switzerland, in 1993.

Louise Slater

Born: 1956, Wolverhampton, England
Died: 1999
Education: 1976–79, Sheffield City Polytechnic, England; 1975–76, Walshall School of Art, England

After studying silversmithing and jewelry, Louise Slater developed a strong interest in non-precious materials. In the early 1980s, Slater captured the spirit of the time in her jewelry created from brown paper, sealing wax, and ribbons. She then turned to ColorCore Formica, a material that lent itself well to her preference for a palette of bright colors. The resulting jewelry was an instant success and gained the British Design Award in 1988. Slater was strongly influenced by Asian art and design, notably that of Japan and Thailand, where her parents lived and where she frequently visited.

In 1986, Slater expanded her range of objects to include mobiles, which were sold at the Guggenheim Museum in New York, among other places. At the time of her death, she was working on an exhibition of new work for a gallery in Tokyo.

Emmy van Leersum

Born: 1930, Hilversum, The Netherlands
Died: 1984
Education: 1962, Konstfack Skolan, Stockholm, Sweden; 1958–62, Instituut voor Kunstnijveer heid sonderwijs (later renamed Gerrit Rietveld Academie), Amsterdam

While studying jewelry design in Amsterdam, Emmy van Leersum met fellow student Gijs Bakker, who became her husband and creative partner for the next twenty years. Together van Leersum and Bakker revolutionized the way people thought about jewelry. Believing that jewelry should promote equality, they rejected traditionally precious materials in favor of aluminum, steel, and acrylic, and they eliminated superfluous ornament in order to break decisively with the tradition of jewelry as unique and precious.

In 1967, the couple dramatically displayed their jewelry using live models in the groundbreaking *Sieraad III* (Jewelry III) show at Amsterdam's Stedelijk Museum. Over her career, van Leersum remained focused on line and geometric form, producing work in small editions. Although she introduced color into her designs in the early eighties, her work remained in keeping with the spirit of rationality and clarity that characterized the Dutch Smooth movement. In 1983, Emmy van Leersum received the prestigious Herbert Hoffmann Prize at the Internationale Handwerks Messe in Munich. Van Leersum created jewelry until her death from cancer in 1984.

David Watkins

Born: 1940, Wolverhampton, England
Education: 1959–63, University of Reading, England
Current Residence: London, England

David Watkins was originally trained as a sculptor. In 1964, he began designing black and white acrylic jewelry and paper jewelry with his wife, Wendy Ramshaw, with the intention of making fashion jewelry based on the Op Art and Pop Art trends in painting at the time. Watkins also made sculpture and enjoyed a career as a jazz and blues musician. In addition, he made many of the models for Stanley Kubrick's film *2001: A Space Odyssey.* Watkins credits the "anything goes" spirit of the era with directly influencing his later work as a jewelry artist.

In the early seventies, Watkins began designing bold neckpieces of colored acrylic with gold or silver that were inspired by his studies of the relationships between geometric and linear forms and the human body. In 1984, Watkins accepted the position he currently maintains of Professor and Head of Department of Goldsmithing, Silversmithing, Metalwork and Jewellery at the Royal College of Art in London. Watkins continues to work in a variety of media and forms, always retaining his interest in designing jewelry that can be worn.

BIBLIOGRAPHY

British Crafts Centre. *Jewellery Redefined: The 1st International Exhibition of Multi-Media Non-Precious Jewellery* (exh. cat.). London: British Crafts Council, 1982.

British Crafts Council. *The Jewellery Project: New Departures in British and European Work 1980–83* (exh. cat.). London: British Crafts Council, 1983.

Broadhead, Caroline. *New Tradition: The Evolution of Jewellery 1966–1985* (exh. cat.). London: British Crafts Centre, 1985.

Cartlidge, Barbara. *Twentieth-Century Jewelry.* New York: Harry N. Abrams, 1985.

Cartlidge, Barbara. *Celebrating Electrum's 25th Anniversary: The Innovators.* London: Electrum Gallery, 1996.

Ewing Gallery of Art and Architecture. *Jewelry-Means-Meaning* (exh. cat.). Knoxville, Tenn.: Ewing Gallery of Art and Architecture, 1988.

Dormer, Peter, and Turner, Ralph. *The New Jewelry: Trends and Traditions.* London: Thames and Hudson, 1985.

Drutt, Helen W., and Dormer, Peter. *Jewelry of Our Time: Art, Ornament and Obsession.* New York: Rizzoli, 1995.

Falk, Fritz, and Holzach, Cornelie. *Schmuck der Moderne 1960–1998: Bestandskatalog der modernen Sammlung des Schmuckmuseums Pforzheim.* Stuttgart: Arnoldsche, 1999.

Frum, David. *How We Got Here: The 70s, The Decade That Brought You Modern Life.* New York: Basic Books, 2000.

Halsey, A. H., and Webb, Josephine, eds. T*wentieth-Century British Social Trends.* New York: St. Martin's Press, 2000.

Harrod, Tanya. *The Crafts in Britain in the 20th Century.* New Haven, Conn.: Yale University Press, 1999.

Hooker, Mark T. *The History of Holland.* Westport, Conn.: Greenwood Press, 1999.

Johnson, Paul, ed. *Twentieth-Century Britain: Economic, Social, and Cultural Change.* Harlow, Essex: Addison Wesley Longman, 1994.

Joris, Yvonne G. J. M., ed. *Broken Lines: Emmy van Leersum 1930–1984.* The Hague: Gegevens Koninklijke Bibliotheek, 1993.

Joris, Yvonne G. J. M., ed. *Jewels of Mind and Mentality: Dutch Jewelry Design 1950–2000.* Rotterdam: Het Kruithuis, Museum of Contemporary Art, 2000.

Klein, Richard. *Jewelry Talks: A Novel Thesis.* New York: Pantheon Books, 2001.

Kransen, Charon, ed. *Point of View: Dutch Contemporary Jewelry and Design* (exh. cat.). New York: Charon Kransen, 1990.

Larsen, Helge, ed. *Cross Currents: Jewelry from Australia, Britain, Germany, and Holland.* Sydney: Museum of Applied Arts and Sciences, Power House Museum, 1984.

Lewin, Susan Grant. *One of a Kind: American Art Jewelry Today.* New York: Harry N. Abrams, 1994.

Nehring, Neil. *Flowers in the Dustbin: Culture, Anarchy, and Postwar England.* Ann Arbor: University of Michigan Press, 1993.

Newton, Gerald. *The Netherlands: An Historical and Cultural Survey 1795–1977.* London: Ernest Benn Limited, 1978.

Phillips, Clare. *Jewelry from Antiquity to the Present.* London: Thames and Hudson, 1996.

Rodrigo, Evert. *Concepts Comments Process: Dutch Jewellery 1967–1987.* Amsterdam: Rijksdienst Beeldende Kunst, 1987.

Schama, Simon. *The Embarrassment of Riches: An Interpretation of Dutch Culture in the Golden Age.* New York: Random House, 1987.

Stedelijk Museum. *Mag het iets meer zijn? Marion Herbst 1968–1993.* Wijk en Aalburg, The Netherlands: Pictures Publishers, 1993.

Steiner, Christopher B. "Rights of Passage: On the Limited Identity of Art in the Border Zone." In *The Empire of Things: Regimes of Value and Material Culture.* Santa Fe, N. Mex., School of American Research and Oxford: James Currey Ltd., 2001.

Turner, Ralph. *Jewelry in Europe and America: New Times, New Thinking.* London: Thames and Hudson, 1996.

Van Elteren, Mel. *Imagining America: Dutch Youth and Its Sense of Place.* Tilburg, The Netherlands: Tilburg University Press, 1994.

Walgrave, Jan. *The Ego Adorned, 20th Century Artists' Jewelry.* Antwerp: Koninginfabiolazaal, 2000.

Watkins, David. *The Best in Contemporary Jewellery.* Mies, Switzerland: Rotovision, 1993.